for Geoff and Joan

with good memories of

birds and Shedfield

if not of Duchess..

Richard Ash

April 2009

A Light on Shore

By the same author

The Royal Navy Today and Tomorrow (1983)
Anit-Submarine Warfare (1984)
British Sea Power in the 1980s (1985)
Maritime Strategy for Medium Powers (1986)
Air Defence at Sea (1988)
Arms Control at Sea (1989)
The Oxford Illustrated History of the Royal Navy (General Editor) (1995)
The Prizes of War (1998)
War at Sea in the Ironclad Age (2000)
Lewin of Greenwich (2000)
Maritime Britain (2005)

A Light on Shore

by

Richard Hill

The Memoir Club

© J. R. Hill 2009

First published in 2009 by
The Memoir Club
Arya House
Langley Park
Durham
DH7 9XE

British Library Cataloguing in
Publication Data.
A catalogue record for this book
is available from the
British Library

ISBN: 978-1-84104-197-1

Jacket design from a painting by John Webster RSMA
Typeset by TW Typesetting, Plymouth, Devon
Printed by the MPG Books Group in the UK

Dedication

For my family and friends: *Mason's Yard*, p. 78

Contents

List of Illustrations ix

Preface xi

Chapter 1   Juvenilia 1

Chapter 2   Sea Time 14

Chapter 3   Professional Navigator 32

Chapter 4   Whitehall Warrior 45

Chapter 5   Three Sea Pieces 63

Chapter 6   Middle Temple and After 71

Chapter 7   A Light on Shore 98

Chapter 8   Epilogue 105

Index of Titles 106

Index of First Lines 108

List of Illustrations

Between pages 50–51

1 'Shining girl' (p. 36). Richard and Tricia, 21 July 1956.

2 Editing, 1944–2002: not shown are the Middle Temple Newsletter and the *Oxford Illustrated History of the Royal Navy*.

3 HMS *Cardigan Bay* 'Compass Platform Personalities': Captain Nigel Pumphrey surrounded by Lieutenants Richard Hill, Lewis Payne, Peter Kimm. Cartoon by Lieut. (now Captain) Peter Kimm.

4 'All the bright destroyers' (p. 70): 5th Destroyer Squadron, 1961. From bottom HM Ships *Duchess, Diamond, Crossbow, Diana, Battleaxe.*

5 (Top) Amateur theatre, a London pastime with the Old Admiralty Dramatic Society, often as Universal Understudy. In this production of *Rope* (1964) I think I stepped in with a fortnight to go. Luckily I was a quick study. From left Marjorie Imlah, Alan Brookes, Chris Young, Doug Munson, Richard Hill, Clifford Snell, Joan Walsh.
(Bottom) A spare Flag Officer Gosport-side was always useful for Divisions: inspecting the guard at HMS *Daedalus*, 1981.

6–7 'Green things springing' (p. 97). Clockwise from top left, Lucy and Harriet Hill; Nigel Hill; Tricia, Lucy and Harriet; Eleanor Callcut; Charlotte Thistlewood; Alexandra Callcut; Anna Thistlewood; Richard with Penny Callcut; James Thistlewood.

8 (Top) The family commissioned this cartoon by Charles Miles for my 60th birthday. It looks a bit overdone, but life at the Middle Temple was indeed full of varied interests, as well as a fair whack of work at the day (and sometimes night) job.
(Bottom) Humphrey Lyttelton and his band played at the Middle Temple every year. His lightning cartoon for Tricia crowned one occasion with extra delight.

Preface

Verse, and a Life

I have produced about ten published books, and quite a few bits of books, not to mention conference papers and other wordy things, mostly knocking about in libraries or archives somewhere. So it is a fair question whether I should go to press, one more time, at 80 or so. But as a wordsperson, which for better or worse I am, there are still some words around, both on paper and in my head.

They are, moreover, different from anything I have previously published, since they take the form of verse, and some of this does seem to me (of course I am partial) to merit preservation. It may mostly be, as much poetry has always been, a different way of expressing the obvious, a light cast from a new angle on familiar objects or situations; yet even that may catch the imagination and help to liberate the spirit, somewhere, sometime.

Most books of poetry simply display their wares without any surrounding material, as though they were gems without a setting. This is quite surprising, when you come to think of it; a poem that stands entirely by itself is a rare creation, and most poems that I have read do not pass the test. So the pieces that follow will mostly be set in the circumstances in which they were written, and to that extent what follows is an autobiography.

Yet it is not by any means a full account of my life. There will not be very much about my work as a naval officer, administrator or historian (though references to it come into many of the poems); such information and opinions and, perhaps, wisdom as I have gathered in those fields is in my other books and papers. They belong to the world of prose where facts matter, proof is necessary and clarity is essential. That was the main part of my work as a wordsperson, what I was paid for in fact; it may have been useful in its time, and some of it may serve historians in the future. But it is not meant to be art, nor to have the permanence of art. Poems, however modest, do have that aspiration.

I have, too, been sparing with the details of personal and family life, relating them on the whole to the poems. Maybe there should have been more. But, to be honest, and having seen a lot of naval autobiographies over the years, I am not convinced that the detail is of compelling interest to most readers, and the poems do sometimes illuminate what happened in a way that prose might not.

I have allowed myself to write, in the commentaries on some of the poems, of the technicalities of their construction. This is mostly because such things are of great interest to me, and were the product of very intense thought and internal argument. Will this subject, this image or contrast of images, sustain a couple of verses? Or a sonnet? Or will it be so complex as to need more comprehensive (and therefore more difficult) organisation? Readers who are not interested in such things will be well advised to skip those bits and just read the local colour and the verses.

The sequence of the book will largely follow the course of my life, which is less untidy than any other. There will be minor distortions, caused by the lappings of memory and revision. Wordsworth is my least favourite major poet, but his 'emotion recollected in tranquillity' is a pretty accurate formulation of the process, and recollection can take a long time and tranquillity can be hard to come by. Inevitably, therefore, each poem will be set in the context not only of the time it was written, but – if it is relevant – of the event that generated it, even though those may be some years, even decades, apart.

It is conventional say something about one's background. Well, it was slightly lower than middle-middle class, and contained many ingredients for success: an intelligent, talented and ambitious mother who thought she had married beneath her; a steady, gentle father in a secure official job; and I was quite bright and got a scholarship to the Royal Naval College, at the height of the Second World War, following a calling to the sea from an early age. The College at Dartmouth was bombed shortly before I was due to join, and was evacuated first to Bristol and then to Eaton Hall, Chester. In consequence many of the archaic rules that had governed pre-war Dartmouth vanished; there was no 'genius of the place' any more. Moreover, our naval supervisors were seasoned men resting after rigorous sea and war service, different from the ambitious careerists we might have encountered earlier; and academic ability was recognised, under a new and wise headmaster. This suited me well: I was a lucky fellow.

RICHARD HILL
Bishop's Waltham, 2009

CHAPTER 1

Juvenilia

The Parnasse

I WROTE AN AWFUL LOT of verse at the Royal Naval College and it
still knocks around in a box somewhere, but this sonnet looks to
be the only thing worth preserving. I find it surprising that I wrote
it at 16, but on inspection it is much less mature than it tries to be.
The first line must have owed a lot to Housman (*The chestnut casts his
flambeaux, and the flowers . . .*); but after the second, it does take its
own course. What it says about the Parnassiens is probably inaccurate.
But with a sideways look at Verlaine and Mallarmé, perhaps my
strictures were not too ill-founded.

There is one structural oddity. The usual Petrarchian sonnet
divides into an eight-line and a six-line section, but in this one the
eighth line leads into the finale. I suspect this was because I couldn't
handle the pure form, but it may have produced a legitimate variation
on the pattern, and you will find another, more deliberate, one near
the very end of this book.

The lotus caught your daytime, and the flowers
Lie scattered in the paths on which you tread.
The sunset rose blooms a far duskier red
When you are there to watch the evening hours.
And, in return, you give us the bright towers
Of sensuous verse: and how Hjalmar bled
And the faun dreamed, we know: this you have said.

But when the shadow of the Real lowers
Across your threshold, and your vagrant schemes
Are troubled with a tremor of the pen,
And you are sorely tempted to dissect
The vacant thoughts of your heroic men –
Why then, I pray you, go on with your dreams
Nor waste your waking thoughts with intellect.

Fear

I went to sea in 1946, and this sonnet is the first of my poems that has to do with the sea. It came from experience; boatwork was part of a midshipman's life, both weather and the acquisition of professional skills were constant challenges, and responsibility really was there from the beginning. I don't think this is much of a sonnet; its structure is lazy, with a cop-out in the rhyme-scheme of the second quatrain, and the language is pedestrian, but perhaps it is lifted by the sudden shift of image in the last two lines.

Twice I have seen his face within a wave,
Once on a night of storm, and once in sun
That steeped the sea in gold: I saw him run
Before my bow, and I had dug my grave –
But worse, the clutching at my craven soul
That these with me, as well, would surely drown
In struggling terror, going down and down
Forever, where the stubborn waters roll.

This was the deadly fear, that through my sin
They too would fail, and throw their arms aloft;
They too would see the wolf-waves rushing in,
And know my words of courage were but lies,
As on snow-ridden uplands, with no croft
In sight, men, numbed, lie shouting at the skies.

Greenwich

An enlightened Admiralty sent us, after sixteen months' time as midship-men, to the Royal Naval College at Greenwich to be de-barbarised and taught, by supervisors of singular quality, a modicum of culture and (as one said) the principles of the Good Life. We had two terms of this privileged existence; they were spacious days. I wrote a tremendous amount of verse during this time, bashed out on an old Remington portable. It was described by an aged professor as 'rather like an excess of wind', and he was not wrong, but a few truer notes survive, and my experiments with verse-forms, particularly when handling more complex subjects, were a significant development.

Prayer

Eliot was, of course, read and re-read at this time, and inevitably, following *The Waste Land*, Frazer as well. So much of my stuff was seasonal and heavy with rites of spring and autumn. Less tedious were some of the shorter poems on this track, and this one shows an unusual feature in having the slowest two lines (the sixth and seventh) I have ever written. Technically, I believe, they are a three-foot spondee followed after two short beats by a four-foot spondee. The sentiment may be ordinary, but there is some weight in the language.

There is always the fear
At the half-shrouded dying of the year
That spring will come no more.
Always the terror and propitiation
Always the elation
When the last frost lifts, when the last hoar
Frost lifts from the fields.

When the soul yields
Let it be summer, and the sun on the windowpane,
And small lethargic beetles boom
Around the corners of my room –
Let me see down the lane
To the green where white figures come and go,
Till they slow
And fail in the failing umber,
Turning to ghosts without number,
White as the cold snow.

Sunset on London River

No one could fail to be moved by the dignity and grandeur of the Royal
Hospital Buildings at Greenwich, and by their situation on the south side
of the Thames. We all spent some time at the railings by the river – still
there 60 years later – taking in the scene, at one time or another. In this
poem, I don't know what the crowds were waiting for; as will be seen later,
the idea of a press of humanity recurred.

The slow
Unbroken rhythm of the conch laps
On the beach. The barge's foresail flaps
Untended in stays.
Under the glow
Of this unbelievable evening the river prays
For us, preys
On us. Behind the black pillars of the powerhouse
The sunset makes carouse
With a surfeit of colour, the river swirling
Blood and gold.
Streamers of smoke curling
Formally among tangled clouds
Have never told
To the waiting crowds
Such a tale of wistful wonder,
To the deep river under
The bridges, have never made
Such a pattern of twisted skeins.
The last ghost has been laid,
Nothing remains,
For the moment, but the sublime
Mind out of time.

Grey Morning at Greenwich

The theme of Christopher Wren's architectural masterpiece is taken up in
this sonnet, but all too soon, I fear, is overlaid by some rather cheap
philosophy. It suggests that we did do some work in those eight months,
and even occasionally found it testing; equally, that we realised there would
soon be more arduous times ahead, to which most of us looked forward
with relish. As far as the first line is concerned, I had and still have no idea
whether the chimes of the clock at Greenwich are in the Dorian mode or
not; it made a good first line. I was only 19.

A stately figure in the Dorian mode
Chimes through the window. Grave and calm the tone
Of the white pillars with their heavy load
Of pediment and frieze, the overgrown
Black of London. Even here, no rest
Is on the suppletinted earth; no time
Is timeless, and the wanton angry test
Of each day causes discord in the chime.

I'd have it so. The resting moment waits
But has no splendour in its afterglow;
There is no further hill beyond the gates,
No other footprint trampled in the snow.
But striving, at a turn we can retrieve
The rapture of the moment, and believe.

For a Parting

Falling into and out of love was, inevitably, part of existence at Greenwich, and most of the lyrics written at that time have mercifully disappeared or linger at the bottom of a box. This survivor is chosen because it has a certain coherence. It is more serious in tone than the event warranted; but I never did see her again.

When we have said goodbye
I do not want to see your face again;
No flicker from your eye
Nor your white signals fluttering from the train.

When the last words are done
I must not let your shadow come once more
Between me and the sun:
But listen for the closing of the door.

When the last moment's past
And you set out towards your certain day,
Show then that you were cast
In a true mould, of fine and simple clay;

And let this be your pride
In after years: into that well of sound
You walked with easy stride
And, though your heart bid you look, did not look round.

Ultima Thule

It is always easier to write gloomy than joyous verse, and that applies
however old or young one is. This may be thought one of the gloomiest,
and quite unsuited to a young man at the threshold of a varied and fulfilling
life. But there it was, and the imagery was strong in my mind, and I think
it comes through on to the page.

When on the Gulf Stream of our richer years
We have floated, and the bergs begin to close,
Scending and shifting down the coast of Labrador
Till spray gives way to the swell of remembered hopes and fears
And a redeyed sunset glows,
At last we shall drift to a place the ancients knew before.

There, in flat calm, the waters slide relentless
Over the earth's green sill.
Eddy and churn and whirlpool
Circle around low islands of grey marl
Where nothing grows: soundless and scentless,
Grey and still.
Then receding
Down the sealane like a dark corridor
With the world at the end growing diffuse and dim,
The tug of the tide swirling and leading
On, till we drift without an effort more
Over the rim.

Final Movement from 'A Consort of Viols'

At the same time as writing the shorter poems, I was occupied in trying to treat larger themes. It seemed to me that this needed a rigorous approach in order to avoid meandering off in an aimless way (perhaps our staff-course training, with its insistence on 'the selection and maintenance of the aim', had an influence). In any case, what I was in effect doing was rejecting the romantic principle with its insistence on a free-flowing, single-issue pattern and embracing the classical ideal of contrast, juxtaposition and harmonious comparisons. This would not necessarily lead to tidy conclusions, but it would at least impose discipline on what might otherwise be a jumble of images and forms.

The structure I chose as a preferred model was that of the musical sonata. As I understood it, this could be summarised as, for the first movement, first subject – bridge passage – second subject – development – recapitulation – coda; for the second movement, *either* main subject – episode – main subject, *or* theme and variations; and for the final movement, a rondo bringing in the main subject at least three times with contrasting passages between. An extra movement, typically lying third and consisting of scherzo – trio – scherzo *da capo* – was an option, seldom attempted.

How all this could be worked in words was the trick. Clearly it could not too precisely follow the musical format; music consists often of exact repetition of previous matter, and is satisfying as such, partly because the listener wants to hear it again and partly because the intervening material gives the repetition new meaning and depth. That does not work with poetry except to a very limited extent, perhaps in the use of refrains or motto-themes. However, where it does seem to work, or did for me, is in the recurrence or re-treatment of subject-matter, particularly after the presentation of contrasting material. The linking of one group of images, based upon one subject-set, with another group provides – or should, if the thing is skilfully managed – a satisfying whole.

The relatively long poem which follows is an example of how I tried to tackle this structure. It is a final-movement form, that is to say a rondo. The main theme is the narrative of the old guide to the ruined city, and there are three intervening passages which take the form of choruses; the first and third are the voices of the city's (long dead) inhabitants and the second that of the visiting (time) travellers. Technically this is, I think, a sonata–rondo but that is not important. The other three movements were, in my view, not worth preserving.

As to the subject-matter, that was heavily influenced by two factors. The first was my own experience of London at the time. 1948 was a grim year. The Second World War had taken a lot out of the British people: they were tired, many were depressed, some exhausted almost; food was still generally rationed; much bomb damage had not been repaired; grime, and often smog, was endemic. Steps had been taken on the climb back to peace and prosperity, but it was a long way uphill. The second factor was a book, Lewis Mumford's *The Culture of Cities*, which I had chosen as a prize (Science – Division II) on passing out of Dartmouth. Mumford was an American liberal visionary, putting forward concepts of social organisation based upon city and regional planning that were, on their face, highly attractive; one wonders what he would have thought now of Caracas or Sao Paolo. Even in 1948 I could not bring myself to envision Mumford's idealised world as being in the future; the time-travellers in *A Consort of Viols* come from a lost region in the past. Their chorus, in the middle of the movement, has in retrospect quite a strong Marxist tone; but perhaps it is, more simply, nostalgia for an age that never existed.

Visitors come here often from the lost region,
Forward in time only. They are frightened sometimes
But I can tell them these ruins hold no ghosts;
Those that lived here were not, shall I say,
Lasting ghost material. I will guide you
If you wish it so.

There, over there where the ravens are wheeling –
Please do not climb on the masonry. It is unsafe,
The walls are heavy and solid, the foundations
Were much too shallow – there, as I say, they watched
Gladiatorial games. No, not so much glorying
In the players' skill as their own unhinged release
From the obvious bonds. Some sixty thousand, I'm told,
Roaring as one. I often wonder as
I sit by the fire of an evening, if there were any
Who watched the crowd instead of the game;
The rulers could hardly miss such an unaltering
Study in social wisdom. But I wander again,
You will forgive an old man havering in a dead city.
That bridge with its girder tiptilted upward,
Fine lines, and strong in its day – There, it's said, they went
In their thousands through the grey evenings
Toward their sleeping place. It seems that near the end
Faces were so alike that only by
Their uniforms could one identify;

And all quite quiet. Talking was left to traffic
And orders from loudspeakers. We have one still,
A rare exhibit; I will show you later
If it interests you.
                         Here in this ventriloquist hall
Assemblies were held. Shout and hear the echo;
It may be distorted; strange things have been heard here.

Who shocked the rafters
With the clean shout of a bygone age?
Who intrudes now on our
White silences? We have earned silence.
When the din ceased
At half past six and only puffing trains
And late carousers beat into our rest,
Then we could sleep: malcontent thoughts
Idled through frozen marshes of mind to be lost
In the weary rustle of falling leaves.
One evening was very like another;
We were chilled at first but soon
Found each his fantasy; settled down
Into routine, broken only
By Sundays and marriages, funerals and Christmas;
Each had its pattern, set and preordained,
Despising logic. Life was easier thus,
Knowing where one stood. But always there was noise:
The same noise at the same time, though sometimes
Unexpected shocks came crashing
Through cardboard walls. Now even when
We sleep so soundly, noise still
Is conceived and brought forth.

No sir, no ghost, but the toiling of the wind
Through the burst walls yonder. This way, if you please,
We have much ground to cover. The city is big;
Small beginnings gave it a firm foundation,
The roaring years followed. Like a booming river
It broke its walls and flowed faster than glaciers
Over the marshes. More and more was added,
Built up and outward; the social rhythm changed,
The packed throngs grew less rowdy as control

Passed from them, but increase went on until
Like an overloaded nucleus the place exploded.
That was an evil hour. The crowd that had learned
To act as one, went mad as one; the life they lived
Was worth no expense of air. They ceased to breathe,
Having no will to live. Go carefully here, please.
This is the burial ground, a place full of pitfalls.
You are advised to sing; it is lonely here
And thoughts fly black across the south transept
Darkening the sun.

In our lost region
The nave of trees
Blackens the sun
But dapple shadows
Denote that light
Is present and one
With the sobering dark.

On the common land
At midnight, torches
Pick their triumphant
Way through bracken
While the home farm
Gives friendly shelter
To wayworn weary
Travellers.

And the day through
The sky remains
High above us,
With clear horizon
And dark against
The dovegrey sunset
Lateshocked sheaves
Show our fulfilment.

In our lost region
The drought of summer
The frost of winter
Are living totems;
Our struggle unceasing

Our end unending,
Travail our heritage,
Its labour our joy,
Its joy our birthright.

It is strange how, among the ruined building,
The rotten concrete and the rusted girders,
These stones stay young. Their curt inscriptions remain
While the papyrus moulders and the yellow lichen
Blanks out the pediment. Strongly enough
They built this last dormitory, and saved against
A pauper's funeral. The sun is well across
The meridian now; we must move on.
These twisted tracks were straight once, and creatures of steel
Seeming more alive than those that served them
Fared down them, drawing the staring people
Hither and thither, day after day. The rhythm never tired,
Planning perfected hauled them in safety
From nowhere to nowhere. Life ran on wheels
Smooth and ordered. These, some think, were their deities,
Day to day arbiters of destiny,
Little tin gods on wheels. And, as even the most
Subservient will escape, the runaway train,
Crossing points the wrong way, harming none
Though careless of others, has a noted place
In their mythology.
                    Perhaps this was
The most strange sight of all, the hurrying figures
At morning, the tired ones at evening, moving
Through this hall and the barriers beyond,
Faces impassive, feet like fire, and thought
Unuttered, hardly realised at all.

Oasis in the stone desert,
Where are your palms now, where your mirage-making
Water? Sweet river hold us,
Gently enfold us in your downbreasted dovegrey stream:
Peace, peace now, and no more hurry
To a zero hour.

Alone
Here among faces familiar but unknown

That see what we do and yet know nothing of us,
Alone
In the teeming archway
Packed with passive faces
Like our own.

We are one yet sundered.
Oh grey stone desert of rock that flows
Like lava over the washed bodies of souls
Leave us at least a caravan to travel
With, a burning hand to hold our burning
Hands, a cracked voice crying from the cactus
That we are known, cared for,
Not left to die alone.

Strange indeed, this passing of active into passive
Apathy besetting this almost forgotten people.
We near our journey's end. You will not forget, you
Voyagers through the dark country, you will remember,
I hope, what you have seen. I am always glad,
I the old caretaker of a ruined city,
To welcome you. Here where death has at last
Come to the end of striving because the victory
Is complete, because the plan went forward
Without a check, here is a place to recall
Heavily when the lost region welcomes
Your faces again. I am old and not overwise,
But I have heard of your country and wish you well.
Though you have seen the symbols of corruption
You have not felt its force. Now, I suppose,
You will go backward in time. Thank you. Good night.
Remember the old man in his shack on the hill
Watching over the bones of a city that died
Finding no cause to live.

CHAPTER 2

Sea Time

AFTER GREENWICH, IT WAS TIME to go to sea as a professional officer with a stripe on my arm to suggest the passage from the equivocal status of midshipman – still very much a learner, but with some authority and responsibility, a position long recognised by the Royal Navy as valuable not only to the individual but to more senior officers and ship's company alike – to that of an executive. At first, as acting sub-lieutenants, we did not hold the royal commission, but were expected to act as though we did and, if gaps occurred through sickness or temporary absence of our seniors, were given considerable responsibility both operationally and administratively.

That was followed, in 1949, by a series of professional courses ashore in the Portsmouth area: torpedo and anti-submarine, gunnery, navigation, communications, flying, damage control, combined operations. The theoretical work came fairly easily to me, the practical surprisingly so (except flying, at which I was safe but cack-handed and, to my relief, graded 'unsuitable'). I am not sure that even then I grasped how fundamental to the business of command was one's comprehension of all the essential aspects of warfare and ship management. I think that at our training establishments, especially in the earlier days, we had been given the idea that leadership was a god-given attribute that only the chosen could aspire to, and some part of that lingered for years, even after considerable success in professional training and going to sea to consolidate that success.

Anyhow, as a watchkeeping officer in the Mediterranean Fleet I gained confidence: quite quickly professionally, a good deal more slowly socially. There was still time for the occasional foray into verse; as is usual with memory, the occasions on which I wrote it are largely forgotten, and in many cases the words had been half-formed long before.

Campo

The combined Home and Mediterranean Fleets' gathering in Gibraltar was still a feature of the 1949 navy, and was an occasion for high jinks and mild misbehaviour as well as some serious exercising by the assembled ships, but there was time for excursions across the border into Spain, sometimes solo in my case. Although my midshipman's time in the Far East had given me some insight into more foreign lands, this part of Europe struck some chord I suppose. Torremolinos, by the way, was then a simple fishing village and the whole coast as far as Malaga was almost untouched by tourism.

Yellow land
Red in the evening, green after rain.
Still you stand
Over the border, foothills of Spain.

Limewash houses
Totter with gentility;
Pablo carouses
On a dun beach by the blue sea.

A pretty girl runs
After a green van, American made;
A policeman suns
Himself, finding no shade.

Underfed cows
Malcontent stumble with bells
Around their necks, and browse
Clumps of yellowing grass near near-dry wells.

But over the hill
Comes the sullied half-broken voice of a boy
Who quickens the still
Stricken evening with joy

Because of his tune
That has kept its unanimous chord
With the sky, and the rune
Of the waves, and the broken sword

In the church of the grail,
With the indolent gentle compelling ones
Who know how to fail
And to meet the beat of a thousand suns.

Downs, Dorset

The Portland Naval Base too gave opportunities for wandering off into a
country that later I came to know better – as indeed I did the work of
Hardy, which at the time I had scarcely read. It was always a special place.
This poem was quite unconsciously written in *terza rima*; had I known then
that it was the rhyme scheme of Dante, I might have tried something else.
But it seemed appropriate at the time, and does not look wrong now.

Here are long downs that stretch
Their hands into the sea
Freckled with windblown vetch;

And an old warrior tree
Looks daggers at the carved
Cliffs curving graciously

Round the eroded, starved
And silence-stricken beach.
Here hawthorn bushes, halved

By wind, have taken each
A sculpture to their form;
Twisted El Grecos reach

Tense hands toward some norm
Impalpable, and eyes
Lifted clean through the storm

Turn past the skylark's cries
Into a simple light
Where the lost promise lies
Certain and infinite.

Anchor Watch, Force 9

It was the proud boast of our group of Sub-Lieutenants that we got through our Gunnery Course without firing a shot. On the scheduled days the range at Wembury in Devon was fogbound, and the gunnery firing ship windbound in St Helen's Roads, so we escaped both short-range and full-range firings. It was good for my career probably, because I made my name at Whale Island by writing and directing (for the entertainment of the visiting Ordnance Board) the Drill for the Mark XIX Cow (complete with full milking crew and rake number), which was much more my scene than demonstrating gun-shyness on the range.

Grey shoreline seen through the scud, and waves all tattered,
Broken and bruised by wind and streaked with spray,
Spindrift too in my face, as if it mattered –
God! What a day.

With white yacht hulls the gulls lie in the roadstead,
Take care with landing, stalling in as light
As dandelion seed: secure, not to be ghosted
Away in the night.

Tell me I'm daft and that I'm making leeway,
Tell me I don't think as a seaman ought,
But I'd rather be out and fighting against that seaway
Than here in port.

Spectator

I cannot recall the genesis of this sonnet. Certainly ceremonial and parades figured in our training, but it looks more like a reversion to my preoccupations at Greenwich than anything stemming directly from the drill shed.

Noisy at times and yet quiescent, I
Watch the parade, see the big men march past,
Hear the loud music die to dregs at last.
Cheering a bit as the cavalcade goes by,
Feeling embarrassed as women round me cry,
I am the watcher, nexus of the vast
Untented number that have never cast
A solo throw. I am their single eye.

Yet now, though quiet still, I can recall
– And minded am to try again the same –
Time when the crowd in harness broke its stall,
Put back the thongs of homage and of thrall,
Like a bright god in fire and judgment came:
Grew tired of watching, and assayed the game.

Of Age

I suppose it was incumbent on anyone aspiring to write poetry to produce
something of this sort at such a time. The sentiments seem unremarkable,
as is the language; and if there are contrasts in the form of the poem, they
are the commonplace ones of present and future. However there are a few
lines I quite like, and one word – 'unsought' – that recurs in subsequent
work and is some sort of motto.

The evening is heavy
With a swollen sense of time.
Undiluted now the sunlight streams in
Through carriage windows dusty as a day
In June's high heat. Earth's fullness
Lets us have no hint of barren
Deserts, this day of daffodils.

Tomorrow is tomorrow. Take now
Only the mild polar airstream with its massive
Cumulus rolling solid as icebergs in
From the Atlantic.
Here is the start of summer. Not again
In the year's cycle may the snowdrop bloom;
But as the spring drops back a heavy pain
Bears down the eyelid. Shall we lose the room
Of unsought delight, the garden found by chance?
Will the rise of the sun, the lift as the bows come clear,
Leave the path of glory and dwindle to romance,
Ending as a routine? There lies the fear.
At least there's no clear-cut line, no dropping-point
For the imagination's scarlet chute;
Stiffens gradually the youthful joint,
Slowly, slowly withers the ageing root.

And yet those garrulous voices twist and twine
About my ears: ah shall I get that trick
Halfway between a grating and a whine,
Full of complaint, unfounded, memory-sick?

No, ah no, says the sunset,
Tugging like a child at the reined aorta,
I am young always to those that can see,
Surely you can see?

Oh ay, I can see yet awhile.
I think that I have never seen
The grass of such a vivid green,
And I am sure I never knew
A sky of such consummate blue;
Never the sea so great, yet still,
Never such swelling of the hill:
These things conspire to emphasise
The coming darkness of the eyes.

So rumbles on the wheel
At fifty miles an hour;
Passenger I can feel
No sense of power.

When such moments vanish,
Turn out the light,
Set the clock's hands to zero,
Lie to yourself no more.

Shrewdly the town closes down.
Four hours more and I am twenty-one.
I shall not change; only a symbol will be there,
A faint yellowing of the sun,
More than a hint of summer in the air.

Owl Eyes

There is not much to say about this one, except that it was amended many years after it was written in 1950 to reduce the banality of the original and try to make the sense clearer.

> To those who think but do not care,
> See nothing that they don't observe,
> The night-owl's eyes
> Are not so wise;
> Their stare is a predation-stare,
> Dark-sensitive the optic nerve.
>
> But through the limits of its brain
> The image-seekers still will find
> The night-owl's eyes
> Are passing wise,
> Because their wide stare lives again
> In the still corners of the mind.

Shot Marshes

This is a bit odd, because I have never to my knowledge shot anything that rose from a marsh, nor waited with a wet bottom in a punt for the dawn flight. It's strange that at this time, with a multitude of new experiences and images to excite the faculties, one was so often drawn to write second-hand things.

> Dead in these forgotten marshes
> Fleet water under the moon
> Lie the bones of unclaimed birds.
> With light ripples the wind journeys inland
> But for the rest there is nothing but dead grass
> And a punt moored to a pole in the queasy mud.
> Hours pass with no glimmer
> But the moon's lantern,
> No sound but the waves' distilled
> Scutter along the shore.
> Then toward dawn with a shriek the geese go flying
> To tell us that after all there is life
> In these shot fens.

Landfall

It is much easier, as I think I've said before, to write gloomy than joyous
verse. This one is unusually full of *weltschmerz* even for a 21 year old.
However it does have some flavour, culled from sailors' disillusioned
humour. It is also the first piece of many that owes something to the
business of astronomical navigation – the production of a single position
line, which is the only outcome of a single observation (*pace* some popular
authors, who don't know what they are talking about), is often sought for
hours, even days, and the glimmer of sun was then, before the days of GPS,
much prized. There is also a strong whiff of Malta about the imagery, but
the land is not Malta. It is, as readers will readily grasp, Symbolia.

> With no rudder or sail
> Driven by gale
> Drifted by current, we fought
> Through the winter ocean, till one
> Bare dingy glimmer of sun
> Gave us the line we sought.
>
> We'll make land tomorrow, the pilot said,
> And a cheer went up from tongues half-dead.
>
> In the afternoon, a pale
> Yellow flicker, as frail
> As a dandelion petal, was metal
> To the mind's anvil. We said
> We'll anchor beyond that head
> And in that land we'll settle.

We'll anchor at midnight, the pilot cried,
And we pulled for the head till we nearly died.

In the morning, when it was still,
On the yellow bones of a hill
We sighted a ruined town;
The town was stone
But the streets were bone
And the churches tumbled down.

We'll build it again, the captain smiled,
But he went about like a man defiled.

And not a seaman's skill
On that waterless yellow hill
Could raise one stone upon
Another: no man could do
What the others, passing through,
Had failed to achieve, and gone.

Well, that's the end of our quest, we said,
This is the seed, and the heart and the head,
And we'll hang about here until we're dead.

Noise in the Mountains

I was in a good deal of doubt about including this long and often unsatisfactory poem. It does not even record any actual event, though there is, in the imagined village festival somewhere in central Europe, some mixed-up memory of station leave in Carinthia and later in Malaga in Holy Week. Nor is it a particularly subtle example of the sonata-form that I still tried to use as a discipline, though clearly there are two themes – the village festival and the commuter existence – which contrast and interact, bound together by the presence of the tourist who is, presumably, a temporary fugitive from the city. Nevertheless the poem has its moments, and does represent a stage in development.

There is noise in the mountains
Challenging wind, and over
The cry of plover;
Singing to ape the strains
Of the leaves' stage-whisper
And thump of drum and horn
Saying a world is born.

There is noise in the rushing valley
Where tourist hotels
And cattle-bells
Jostle for place in the intricate line of sound;
Here voices are trying a canzonetta
And in limpid air a note
Is passed from throat to throat.

Sound runs through the staid procession
Like a small child in joy;
Animates every choirboy.
One expects a secession
From grace, a note hung and held in ambush
Among painted houses, a streamer
Of rapt cadenzas to pleasure a redeemer.

But the throng goes onward to a new enshrining,
A separate spirit in stone
That is the village's own;
The crowd goes forward with brightwork shining
To its known harbour
Silent: the old ways wend
To an appointed end.

From upper windows
Behind lace curtains
Tourists are watching
This strange ceremony.
Their polite amusement records
One single slip,
Small boy out of step,
One tawdry banner;
The mute Madonna
Tells them in tones
Of low compassion
Her considered opinion.

They come from another country.

Round the periphery of Trafalgar Square
Paddles the merry-go-round of passers-by
With a grasshopper jump past the waiting snouts of buses
And a determined drive through defended sectors
Into the hinterland of Charing Cross.
Down back streets to the eastward there is hurry
And threads unite with an uncommon purpose
Into the housebound whole.

But in that undignified
Silent procession
There's no infant
Prodigal joy;
Only an aged
Greymind person
Spreading tired hands
Down a lined face.

Here and there,
A light for a moment flashing
On these dark waters
Is a live one, a loving or loved one,
A being certain that it cannot die
Because it is glad. But these pass
Like a light on a rock unknown
Passed by a ship without a compass:
A useless fixing-mark
Flickering in the middle of darkness.

Flickering in the middle of darkness
Votive candles are
A simile on a star;
There is noise in the high mountains
Living, a scutter of feet on dusty pavement,
Taborpipe and drum
Saying a world has come.

Lamps are out
In the rooms above;
Tourists are trying
To sleep in the shouting darkness.

The village is one. Down the twilight street
Dancers advance;
Rhythms, by chance
As it seems, are beating the softest heartbeat;
Torches flare over the tapping feet
Of an overgrown child
With delight gone wild.

In the rooms above
Six no trumps
Have been bid and played
And gone one down.

The village is one. From each single swayed head
Of laughing man and maid
Sweating and undismayed,
Goes a common ray, a single sun the target
Of the eyes' line of sight. The network
Of thought is complete,
In phase the pulsebeat.

In the rooms above
Two from the festa
In quiet clothes enter;
Say the undisciplined
Dance, and the faces
Shining in torchlight,
Were hardly of interest,
Exhausting to watch.
Two in quiet clothes

Discuss the morrow's
Sightseeingfest
In bored voices.

There is noise in Trafalgar Square.
Starlings at midnight startle the air
With aimless chatter and the unthinking
Round of traffic grates gears.
Here there is no sleep
For the rattle of windy hammers on the tramlines
The footsteps of the late ones
Wandering to their houses.

White
Impersonal light
Sheds on the straggling
Early workers,
Late carousers;
Turns faces to masks.
On the unsleeping city
Grey the day dawns
And in the markets
Wheels are turning.

There is war in the morning
Waged cunningly from rolltop desks
Through the sallyports of typewriters,
Over the aching carcases at Smithfield,
Along the trenches of Welsh coal workings.
From the striving within herself
The city brings forth. Consignments swim
Down tidal reaches toward the leaden estuary,
A hotchpotch in trampers destined
For an uncertain port.

But from a white stone niche high in the mountains
Their Lady watches, making all one
In the moment and throughout time.

After the time of feasting, the dancing ended,
The village is one:
One with the sun
And the raincloud climbing past the glacier;

With the meadows alive with bells of sound and colour;
More than all this, increase
Of an internal peace.

In white tunnels under thundering squares
A disciplined body huddles. But when the train
Draws in, there's striving in those open doorways;
The strongest win. When the clatter begins again
There are no exultant faces thumbing noses
At the windows, only passengers settling down
To a quiet journey through the gathered dusk.
Diverging each toward a barren goal
The occupants of these white paths contend;
The small resultant flutters and is still
Then twitches again. Only confusion stays
From all these forces. This is a world of tensions
And a particular movement either way
Is full of danger.

We are much troubled
By insomnia, though we lie
In beds of comfort.

There is quiet now in the mountains,
The sky gone to sleep
Awaiting the leap
Through the morning's wings on to the stage of day;
The trees gone sober after the day's carousal
Of light and colour;
The river, gone duller,
Now loses the day's extraordinary green, turns grey,
But still, full of sound,
As the current swings round
Beds of pebble and beach of shingle,
Tells that tomorrow is a bright day also.

There is sleep in the village
But stirring under
There live in wonder
The sounds of the evening, unheard yet waiting
In ambush, suspended, uncaptured,
Freer than mountain air
The noise is there.

In the room above
I too am a tourist
But half awake
To the shouting darkness.
My mind in trouble
Turns to the mountains
And finds no rest there
Because I shall never
Be all one with them.

Round the dark monument in Trafalgar Square
No movement is. But under, under the windows,
Staring through the clock of Charing Cross
Is a face of torment, and strife is working under
Our roadways still. The understood world of tensions,
The war in the morning and the mind's unease
Are our background still. Although the mountains give
The sights and sounds, the exterior parts of peace,
We shall never be with them. The sadness of return
To the stricken city is no outcry for mountains
But a regret that after all we may not
Ever completely know them, or be at rest
Under that clouded or this barren sky.

Nuages

This is a deliberately impressionist piece, delivering a succession of half-formed images that contrast the English and Mediterranean landscapes with of course the sea between. I am sure it could be improved but have not tinkered with it.

Over broad acres
Here come and go
Hinds and haymakers
Diligent, slow.

Hay in the meadow,
Grass on the hill,
Sunset and shadow
Determinant still.

Greensleeves remembers
Growth and decay,
Chilleyed Decembers
In middle of May.

—

Mocking birds hover
Swim in the breeze
Suave svelte acres over
Tamarisk trees.

Dolphins are curled
In humorous shapes;
Seas are unfurled
Like bubble of grapes.

Vines are at pressing;
Harvesters cry
A hairy god's blessing
To shout at the sky.

—

Between heat and heaven
Broad acres lie
Growing their leaven–
White branches that fly;

Girding with motion
Grey stallion's hide
That trots on the ocean
Flamboyant with pride;

Between night and day
Sunset or dawn;
Stands in our way
Aphrodite reborn.

That completes my first full tour in the Mediterranean Fleet, which lasted two years and four months. It is striking that not many of the pieces are directly concerned with the sea or the character or business of a ship; as will be seen later, they are more likely to be encountered in retrospect. Nor are they, generally, direct descriptions of the numerous places and things that one saw or experienced. Petra, for example, was memorable (not least for the exploits of the sailors of our party when mounted on horses for the first time in their lives) but got no verses, though I do seem to recall one unsuccessful poem that included the lines *Shadows cast by nothing and / The Khazneh's urn broken.* So memories do often return years later. Perhaps one could call it the transmutation that is an essential part of the poetic process.

CHAPTER 3

Professional Navigator

D URING MOST OF MY TIME in the Mediterranean (1950–52), I was
keen to become a hydrographic surveyor. It gave promise of
being a satisfying specialisation within the naval service, and there was
no doubt about the usefulness of the end-product; I had seen enough
gaps in the charts, and need for amendment, to be sure that what I
would be doing, if accurate and reliable enough, would be of benefit
to seafarers.

What I was less sure about was my own suitability for the work. I
had served in two ships of the Mediterranean Fleet: the cruiser
Gambia and the destroyer *Chevron*, a classic of the genre and the most
beautiful ship in which I ever sailed. I was by now an effective
destroyer officer, alert and knowledgeable on the bridge, adept at
manoeuvring a ship, quick and inventive in the operations room, and
better at relating to sailors (often through shared interest in sport and
ship's activities) than I had expected. Did I have the patience required
to lay down triangulations, arrange sounding routines and tidepole
watching, and draw up fair charts? I had taken away the *Gambia*'s
midshipmen for a sketch survey of Cala Dwejra in Gozo, and that
had been the most tremendous fun resulting in a passable chart, but
I suspected a vast difference between that recreational activity and the
slog of a four-month stint on the sandbanks of the Thames Estuary.

Eventually I concluded that I should stick to and develop what I
appeared already to be good at, rather than move into a field in which
I might prove mediocre or even unsuitable. So, on returning to the
United Kingdom and taking up an appointment to the little frigate
Tintagel Castle, day-running from Portland in support of anti-
submarine training, I volunteered for the Navigation and Direction
branch. This was duly acknowledged within the next sixteen months
by my nomination for a specialist course at HMS *Dryad*.

It was no wonder that some of my verse at this time was suffused
with images drawn from astronomical navigation. In the mid-1950s
that was serious professional business: some electronic aids to

32

navigation did indeed exist, notably radar for coastal work and the Decca and Loran systems for more general position fixing, but they were not always reliable and there were many parts of the world where some of them were not available at all. Observed positions from sights of the sun, moon, planets and stars were an essential part of all ocean passages, and the production of such positions, often under difficult conditions of weather and visibility, was one of the prime satisfactions of the job. Navigators at the beginning of the twenty-first century, with the Global Positioning System at their beck and call, are deprived of that; one hopes they have compensations in other directions.

The First Point of Aries

(That point on the celestial sphere where the plane of the ecliptic crosses the celestial equator)

But, of course, there were other things going on. I had met Patricia Sales at several functions in Portland and Weymouth, and even then – she was, I think, just seventeen at the time – previous flames looked dull by comparison. One day we were talking about some book or other, and I said 'Oh yes, I've read part of that book' – to which she replied 'I don't think there are many books you haven't read part of'. There seemed to be only two options at that point. One was to run like hell, but I chose the other and became more and more attached.

It did not run smooth, of course. Tricia came as my guest to the Coronation Review – where, to my great delight as acting First Lieutenant in the absence of our captain, *Tintagel Castle* looked good and did rather well at cheering – and that was fine, and there were dances and things, but at such a young age, and with university and all sorts of possibilities in front of her, she was understandably in no hurry to cement relationships. So, equally understandably, I got the glooms from time to time and this poem, written in November 1953, was one result.

Astrology is piffle, but the fact is that our birthdays are three days (and seven years) apart at the back end of March, and this seemed as good a hook as any to hang the imagery on. The trignometrical technicalities are, I hope, not too daunting, and the references to the handling of a sextant can be glossed over except by those that 'know

their sky'. As usual in my longer pieces, contrast is evident, but in
this case the interlinkings are more involved and the pattern denser
than before.

> Now that a season of twilight
> Approaches, that mists known before
> As ill harbingers come catfoot
> Over the catspaw sea,
> Now is no time to descry
> Relation twixt x and y,
> It will mean no profit to me;
> Yet, perhaps, I should try
>
> To fit a thought to a star,
> To set a star in gyration,
> To turn that spin to a verse
> To set the verse to a tune,
> Condense the tune to a bar
> And somewhere find the relation
> Between a girl and a moon.
>
> That single constellation
> Under which we were born
> Contains no famous star;
> Something more abstract far
> Is the central point of the horn:
> An immovable reference mark
> In the midst of the dark.
> Here where the sun pushing northward
> Toward the end of winter
> Crosses the frontier, shows his power,
> Here the primal point, the origin of Easter,
> The start of the year –
> Ah raven spring, tear from my heart a song.
>
> But that is far away,
> Beyond tomorrow, before yesterday.
>
> Now that each semitone of autumn
> Bids me beware, each leaf falling
> Tells me take care atop the vaunting pylon:
> Ah too migratory time,
> Too shorn and anxious season

That bears no fruit or flower fit for garland,
You bid me heed because you have seen
Some sorrow of mine before.

Yet, far more personal you,
That make my sleep a stranger,
You saw the leaves, you too
Have sensed the danger
In fitting an act to a reason
A reason back to desire,
In linking desire to a chord
Between a couple of souls;
When in fact the heat of the fire
Had its being because you were bored
And it was the silly season.

No, I shall not admit
To such a poor relation,
Disown this flaccid being
That wanly makes evasion
Into pretence of seeing.
It is a prostitution
Of truth that gives to it
So simple a solution.

My more particular star
Knows no such sudden change;
My more honest mark
Keeps an infinite range.
But oh black constant, First Point of Aries,
Lose that impartial scrutiny for a time,
Look with kindness on this navigator
Seeking position.

How should we, out of the broken twigs of summer,
Form a pattern to last the winter through?
That we have known enough
The splendour and elation
Of minds that make invasion
Of one another . . . stuff
That makes me laugh, makes you
Laugh also . . . this is true.

That we have caught together
A rapture missed apart,
Discussed the angry heart
Widely, if not too well,
Why this is growing weather,
Why should it lead to hell?

He knows, impersonal point
That looks with equal eye
Upon the tyro's clumsy
Clutch at a star, and on
The practised regular swing
Of those that know their sky:
He knows the lexicon
And how all's out of joint
With but one letter missing.

No doubt it would not be new,
The terror and elation
If I were I, you you
And yet we found relation
Between that x and y
To form a true equation.
Then would a song fly high,
A tale both old and true
And certain as the sky.

But now mist takes the sky,
Disowns the sun: horizon
Is sharp and clear no more.
Now the diffuse shapes of autumn
Bid me too known a greeting,
Acknowledge my kinship, too close a relation
To the sad eyes of hares in a frosted field.

I fitted a thought to a dream,
A dream to a curt desire,
Desire to a shining girl,
Lit the girl with my fire;
Now the embers gleam.

The fallacy in the equation
Is somewhere nearer than stars;

The sign that made us close
Yet found no true relation.
Like a serious-minded cheat
I had fudged my altitude;
Instructor will write rude
Remarks on the opposite sheet.

But the sun, halfway through winter,
Has shown an inkling of power;
There may be another hour
That will put this emptiness centuries apart;
Some raven spring may peck a croak from my heart.

The Song of the Over-promoted Cricketer

Cricket had been an abiding passion since early schooldays. Lacking muscular strength, I was not good for much else, though I learned to play passable hockey on a variety of treacherous surfaces and could just about hit a squash ball around the court. But cricket offers opportunities to the under-talented if they are keen enough, and over the years I played quite often in the company of people much more exalted than myself. There was even, in 1948, a match against Cross Arrows *on the square* (well, the very edge of it) at Lord's.

It is a game that thrives on both nostalgia and statistics. I can remember my exact bowling analysis for that match – 10-3-31-1, not too discreditable – and incidents enough, over the years, to bore the pants off any listener. All right, only one: a match in Cyprus against the Oxford and Bucks Light Infantry. Subaltern batting at one end, Regimental Sergeant Major at the other. Subaltern hits a ball towards cover point and calls for an impossible run. RSM roars: 'Get back! . . . Sir'. Subaltern (after regaining ground in flurry of dust): 'My call . . . Sarnt Major.' We loved the Army.

Most of the verse I wrote about cricket has not survived. This was written some years after the events described, to express the feelings of the modest performer.

> Since once on a yellow afternoon
> I hit three fours of purest form,
> Bat sounding the authentic tune,
> Fielders wilting to the storm –
> Though it may never be again,
> Though I fail, ever, to make a run,
> I will still go with the whiteclad men
> That play under the sun.
>
> Since once, by fading evening light
> I bowled a ball that floated past
> A Minor Counties batsman – flight
> And break and length all right at last,
> Though it may never happen more,
> Though I fail, ever, to sound the chords
> Of the timbers' triad, I have in store
> A wicket at Lord's.
>
> Since once, when time was getting late,
> I held a catch from S.M.Brown –

They tell me that he had a date;
At least I didn't put it down –
Though it may never fall to me
To take, ever, a catch again,
I will still play in the company
That comes in from the rain.

Far East, 1954–56

It seems extraordinary that an eighteen months' commission in HMS *Cardigan Bay*, in the Far East of all stations, should have produced no verse to speak of. Certainly there were plenty of other things to do, including my principal job of navigating the ship and, sometimes, squadron; of running the sporting side of the ship; of working with the navies of other nations, including the residue of the Korean War; sometimes, even, of looking after British commercial interests when these conflicted with the security concerns of our closest allies.

The *Cardigan Bay* was a workaday frigate, with a few medium-sized guns, some basic anti-submarine equipment and not very much else to establish her as a warship. But she had a couple of hundred lusty west-country sailors, and they liked nothing better than escorting British merchant vessels, based in Hong Kong, into and out of Foochow and Amoy in the People's Republic of China, past the Taiwanese gunboats – supported by the US Navy – that were based in the offshore islands held, then and now, by the Nationalists. No shot was fired by the *Cardigan Bay*, nor when we were there by the opposition, though it did happen on other occasions.

The *Cardigan Bay* is unique, among the ships in which I have served, in maintaining reunions of the ship's companies throughout the life of the ship – mostly on the Far East station, though her first few years were in the Mediterranean. At those reunions, which happen annually, I expect incidents such as the Formosa Strait Patrol are exaggerated in hindsight. Commonsense prevailed. But they did add spice to an existence that might otherwise have been humdrum.

Towards the end of the commission, inevitably, we put together a ship's magazine, an account of the eighteen months we had spent together under our benign, gallant (three DSOs and a DSC) and much-loved captain, Nigel Pumphrey. Almost inevitably, I was the editor. There was plenty of talent in the ship and we made a fair production of it. The only controversy I remember was over the cover which, naturally, included our ship's crest, a Red Dragon. Our heraldic officer (who later became Hydrographer of the Navy) and expert draughtsman noted that the description of this animal was a 'demi-dragon erased' – which, as he rightly said, meant torn off at the waist. In that case, he added, it should not have a tail. General opinion in the ship was, however, that a tail was aesthetically correct, and anyway the official crest did have a tail.

Our draughtsman was adamant. We should seek heraldic advice. So we wrote a solemn letter to the Somerset Herald at the College of Arms, whose name was Trappes-Lomax. His reply, unfortunately, was too late to be re produced in the magazine itself. But it was to the effect that all the demi-dragons, whether erased or not, that occurred in heraldry remained in possession of their tails. However, went on Trappes-Lomax, if we were not satisfied with this answer, he would start working through the demi-lions.

There the matter rested, and the dragon on the cover of *The Red Dragon* has its tail.

A Sonnet from the East

I suspect that I wrote several pieces to Tricia from the Far East. She may even have kept some of them. One, certainly, I have permission to reproduce because I quoted it at one of her significant birthdays.

I do not say I would not have you change
For we must change in sympathy with time.
I would not lose one moment in the range
That you must traverse, from the happy prime
Of your exultant youth, to fireside-years;
Carnal and mental joys, life's recompense
For some – but few – inevitable tears
To march with wisdom and experience.

Only in one thing I'd not have you alter:
That summer-spirit in you that should stay
Like light around you, stay and never falter
From this immediate to that furthest day.
So you keep this, never shall we be poor;
And I, so rich with this, can ask no more.

The Barnacle Song

For the next few years, as I have said, the Muse almost was absent. I married my 'shining girl' in 1956. There are many records of artists being stimulated by marriage to a great outpouring of work; one thinks of Robert Schumann, and nothing could stop Mozart. Perhaps that is the mark of a true creative talent. But my humbler aspirations were bound up in marriage, a growing family, and in most of my appointments a pretty hectic work schedule.

My time in the aircraft carrier *Albion* (1956–8) did however have one literary aspect. I was the operations room officer and boats' officer: the first not particularly exacting in a carrier, the second a passport to many awkward or embarrassing situations at sea (where it was one of my boats that had to fish ditched pilots out, and quickly – flying in *Albion* was so well-conducted, however, that the need seldom arose) and in harbour (where the opportunities for snarl-ups in both routines and operation were endless).

I was not sorry, therefore, to be volunteered to edit the ship's magazine. It was a quarterly that we called *Albion Angles*, produced on a thing called a Gestetner that required very heavy typing, without a ribbon, into a perforating skin. I spent hours on this machine – no doubt there was help, though I cannot remember much – but the result was a quite lively publication and copies were at a premium on the messdeck.

One production coincided with a passage up-channel to an unscheduled docking to remove growth on the ship's bottom. It supplanted an unwanted visit to Belfast and gave an opportunity for a bit of leave in our home port, and was very popular, and was celebrated in the following verses. Perceptive readers will note a non-rhyme in the first stanza, and also that there is a word that rhymes with 'glass' and means almost the same as 'stern'. I agonised for hours before writing the latter; there was a Royal Personage on board, and I thought I'd better play safe. He'd probably have enjoyed the alternative.

The bottom of the Albion
Started as smooth as glass,
But as the water sauntered on
Past her resplendent stern,
The grim unheeding barnacle,
The swiftly-breeding barnacle,
The flow-impeding barnacle
Said no, it shall not pass.

The Venoms as they landed on
Began to beg and plead
For wind: but we meandered on
At twenty-five; indeed
The shrewd and wary barnacle,
The none-too-chary barnacle,
The rough and hairy barnacle
Was cutting down the speed.

A full power trial in the Straits
Did nothing else but prove
That all at once our bottom-plates
Needed to hit the groove;
The swiftly-growing barnacle,
The sly and knowing barnacle,
The non-close-stowing barnacle
We must, forthwith, remove.

So as our ship's a Pompey ship
And as it's home we wend
We most of us feel fellowship
And, even, call him friend;
The shy and smiling barnacle,
The smugly-piling barnacle,
The sweet beguiling barnacle
That got us Whit weekend.

Exercise Arran Banner

My last commission at sea was in HMS *Duchess* (1960–62). She was nominally a destroyer, but a large and complicated ship that would have been called a cruiser in earlier times. She was also quite fragile, physically and technically, so we had to have our wits about us; and she was also the leader of a squadron, some exactly similar and some of slightly more modest capacity. I was the squadron navigator and operations officer of this lot.

Our Captain (D) was not the most exacting officer in the Navy, but he came close. It was sad that he tried too hard, both to drive us and to generate new ideas; had he relaxed a bit and chosen to do the conventional things well, we would have had a delightful and hugely successful commission, because we abounded in talent and were keen to excel. As it was, everything had to be pushed beyond its limits. One example was Arran Banner, a landing exercise in Pembrokeshire that featured nearly a thousand souls doing some pretty silly things, governed by extremely complex rules of engagement. It is not easy to cover them briefly, but one involved mounting a three-pounder saluting gun in a 27 foot whaler. I described the ensuing rehearsal in the commission magazine . . .

> . . . That bear, however fearfully, the Great Three-Pounder Gun.
> (They tried it in the *Duchess* long before the battle broke,
> And the bows of the whaler were hidden in the smoke.
> Then rose the cheers, huzzah!
> As watchers near and far
> Saw timbers fall and char
> At that Engine's mighty stroke).

The whaler was repaired, and the whole exercise took place as planned; and years later there was some sort of compliment from Captain (D) about my parody of Chesterton. He had been kind enough to recommend me for promotion to commander, and I left the ship at the end of 1962 with the coveted brass hat at the early age of 33, but the sting was that I was on what was called the Dry List, and could not expect a sea command or even to go to sea again. That had its effect later on, as did my time in the *Duchess*, but that is for another chapter.

CHAPTER 4

Whitehall Warrior

S O IN MANY WAYS, AT THE beginning of 1963, it was a new career. I had done a lot of staff work before, particularly in my final sea appointment, so was accustomed to expressing clearly in words quite complicated situations and parameters; but where previously those expressions had generally led to action, now they resulted in assessment, policy and sometimes plans, but seldom operations themselves.

That was most apparent in my first job in the Ministry of Defence, which was to head the Soviet Navy section of the Naval Intelligence Division. It did occasionally involve some supervision of clandestine and surveillance operations, but mostly it was a matter of sorting and assessing the evidence, from many sources, of what the growing and innovative Soviet Navy was up to, and how it might be expected to develop. This is not the place, nor even now would it be right, to describe what we did in any detail, but it is fair to say that the job involved a good deal of travelling to Europe and the USA, and there was sometimes a mild *frisson* that did not amount to danger but, as it were, added piquancy.

The next appointment was to the Imperial Defence College as a member of the Junior Directing Staff. The students were all senior officers, brigadiers and suchlike, from Britain, the Commonwealth and the United States; so for a commander, as I still was, the position was something between dogsbody and *éminence grise*. The Junior Directing Staff's mottoes on tour were 'Never carry their bags' and 'You're bound to lose a few'. It was a privileged situation, though; foreign hosts were eager to demonstrate their strengths and share their problems, often at a very high level. Name-droppers afterwards could claim to have met (for example) Levi Eshkol, Golda Meir, Ezer Weitzman, Abba Eban and even, as a young colonel in a remote kibbutz, Ariel Sharon. And that was just in Israel. As the junior member of a tour, I cast myself as idiot-boy questioner and asked what the more senior dared not. We got caught up in the 1965 Indo–Pakistan War and that tour was curtailed. Given the generally

45

relaxed tempo of the job – with occasional crises or spurts of activity – and the interest of much of it, it is surprising that not much verse came out of it.

That was the case, in reverse, in my next appointment, the West of Suez desk in the Naval Plans Division of the Ministry of Defence. This was extremely busy and the hours were traditionally long, particularly in that period (1967-69) when defence policy was being radically refashioned under Denis Healey and the Navy was going through some painful transitions. I have written about that, in prose, elsewhere. Yet, paradoxically, it was the time when I wrote my most substantial piece of poetry, one indeed that needs a separate chapter (*Three Sea Pieces*) in this account. It had been working somewhere in my mind for years, ever since I left the sea; there will be more about it later, in its place. Apart from that, there were ephemera, often in exchanges across the desk with the officer in charge of NATO business, the delightful, owl-like engineer Kit Baker.

Perhaps this is a point at which ephemera should be discussed. They often seem witty and concise, in their place and at their time, but seldom stay the course, and can be irritating to those who don't know the persons or circumstances involved. I have on the whole excluded them, even when I could remember them.

Then, in 1969, it was back into uniform as executive officer of HMS *Dryad*, the Navigation School and, before 1972 when I left, the School of Maritime Operations. After a period that seemed full of supervising reductions and closures in the Navy generally, it was refreshing to be in a place that was expanding and vibrant. It was busy, and there was little time for versifying, except in after dinner speeches as Wardroom Mess President, when I frequently lapsed into doggerel at the expense of leavers and joiners. That really was ephemeral and has not survived.

At the end of this time I was promoted to captain and began a year's intensive research at King's College, London as a Defence Fellow. I had not been at all sure of my ability to pursue a self-regulated course of study, but it turned out to be within my grasp and produced a piece of work called *The Rule of Law at Sea*. It remained unpublished and was recognised by no academic qualification, but it set the pattern for any later work I did in the legal, analytical or historical fields and was, I believe, useful in setting out the considerations for the application of international law to naval planning and operations – something that had not really been done in depth before. It led to part-time membership of the UK Delegation to the United Nations Law of the Sea Conference. The only success I could claim there was the deletion of four words from a US draft on the regime of Transit Passage – but it did pave the way for the acceptance of that draft by the Conference. Does the course of law pivot on such tiny points?

But there was not much poetry in my academic year, nor indeed in the next four, when I was successively in charge of Naval Future Policy in the Ministry of Defence, and Defence Attaché at the Hague. Both posts were busy and such spare time as there was seemed occupied with other things. Perhaps at this point it is right to discuss the lives we led when appointed to the Ministry of Defence – which amounted to over half the 17 years I spent as commander, captain and commodore.

For most of us, it consisted of occupying pretty basic lodgings in London during the week and going home to the country for the weekend. One's wife was positively discouraged, financially and administratively, from living in London during the week, and lodging allowance would not cover any decent accommodation anyway. So it was a drab existence, worse for the wife than the husband but pretty awful for both, and Friday nights were generally not a happy time. In my final appointment we managed to get a flat in Dolphin Square and that was more civilised (though some sort of subterfuge was needed to make out that we were not living there together, thereby flouting the regulations); but it was an awful time altogether for Tricia, and it is to her utmost credit that she stuck it out.

This is also the right point to introduce the family: Nigel b. May 1959, and Anna and Penny, b. November 1960. Their closeness in age was a singular strain for their mother, less for their father who was off to sea for two years, rotten fellow. In the sixties and seventies they grew into three very interesting, often exciting, individuals. Nigel was independent (he toured south Portsmouth, in a bus, solo, at the age of two and a bit) and has remained so, but in his work for the Hampshire Education Authority, and later for the New Zealand government, has contributed much to the order and economic sanity of public affairs. It was a great sadness that his marriage to Linda did not survive. Anna has adorned the BBC's *Farming Today* for over a decade, and I am not the only one who admires her interviewing technique, less bullying and more effective than some of her peers. She is married to Laurence Thistlewood, fine geologist and bass trombone. Penny quickly acquired the habit of authority, as head of a boarding house where 'boarding need' was redefined during her time there from 'dad in the services' to 'dad in prison', and education in Devon is well served by her and her husband Tony Callcut.

The grandchildren – in order of appearance two Hills, two Callcuts and two Thistlewoods – are a wonderfully diverse set of individuals. One should not make predictions, but from my perspective it would be odd if some of this bright, vivid lot did not at some time or another make us reach for the fireworks and champagne. I am not one of those parents, let alone grandparents, who look for reflections of themselves in their issue, but can still take the most lively interest in their development. May it flourish.

The last MoD appointment, from 1977 to 1979, was on the Defence Policy Staff and in many ways the busiest of the lot, made tolerable only by the interest of the job – a three-way split between The World Outside NATO, Arms Control and the Successor to Polaris – and by my lively, humorous and always inventive tri-service team of policy-makers. From time to time, prompted either by the oddments that came in from other departments (including the Foreign and Commonwealth Office) or by the suggestions of my team, I would spend a few minutes concocting light verses that gave moments of amusement. They were pinned on the wall of the Lieutenant-Colonels' room and ranged from the mildly scurrilous to the frankly libellous and subversive. We called them Wall Posters, after the efforts of the Chinese underground at the time. I am told it did a lot of good for the morale of the Division. I thought quite hard about including them in this volume, but decided to exclude most of them. At this distance of time, they sound a touch patronising, even if the circumstances are memorable, which in many cases they are not. Moreover, what was, or seemed, funny at the time has been overlaid by disasters or tyrannies, affecting the same areas, in more recent news, to the extent that I lifted at least one satirical piece out literally at this moment of writing. But one or two, of the milder sort, do appear later on.

So that was my time as a Whitehall Warrior. People much more senior than me have tended to dismiss their Ministry of Defence work as largely meaningless, simply tinkering with the inevitable processes of government that were decided by civil servants and, sometimes, ministers. I should like to think it was more constructive than that. I think it was Denis Healey who said the chief function of an armed service in peacetime was to survive; and what we in the naval staff tried to do was to ensure that the Royal Navy remained an instrument of sea power that would do what the government of the day told it to do, even if that was not always what current or previous governments had told it to plan for. I have pointed out in other publications the shifts and subterfuges we used to achieve that outcome, and how, so far, we and our successors have just – just – succeeded. The next few years will tell whether it can go on.

A Place

This was written in 1963, in my first year at the Admiralty (soon to be the co-located Ministry of Defence). I suppose the slightly sinister tone was influenced by my job in Intelligence – after all, the first person one met in that Division was the bearded, thickly-Russian-accented Nick Cheshire, guardian of deep memory, scarcely ever committed to paper. Anyway, I did rather like the atmosphere of this one.

Evidently a winter place
With dark still water, mist, pinetrees,
A boathouse on piles, no other habitation.
Flat land: perhaps the Baltic.

Evidently not a dream but a vision,
But so sadly recurring
That I feel I have, not lived, but been cold there:
Perhaps the place of my death.

Conference Hotel

This tries to describe an experience that very many conference-goers – and I was a frequent one from earliest Whitehall times – have undergone. The succession of images will strike differently with submariners, surface sailors and normal people. Take your pick.

For once with time to spare,
To run silent and deep
On this bed, this chair,
Body's or mind's sleep;

For once with no demands
Or cords that tug and whine
At body's or mind's hands:
Slipped from the least line,

Seeking for ease of brain,
Touch of the dove's wing –
Useless. I remain
Tense as a taut spring.

1 'Shining girl' (p. 36). Richard and Tricia, 21 July 1956.

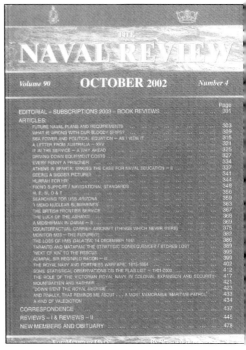

2 Editing, 1944–2002: not shown are the Middle Temple Newsletter and the Oxford Illustrated
History of the Royal Navy.

3 HMS Cardigan Bay *'Compass Platform Personalities': Captain Nigel Pumphrey surrounded by Lieutenants Richard Hill, Lewis Payne, Peter Kimm. Cartoon by Lieut. (now Captain) Peter Kimm.*

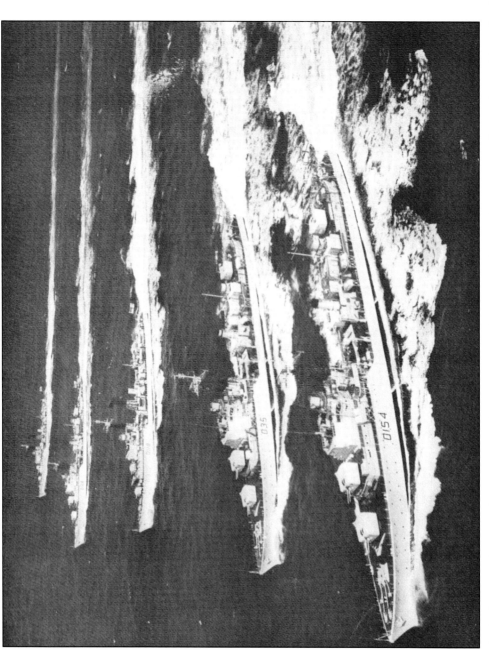

4 'All the bright destroyers' (p. 70): 5th Destroyer Squadron, 1961. From bottom HM Ships Duchess, Diamond, Crossbow, Diana, Battleaxe.

5 (Top) Amateur theatre, a London pastime with the Old Admiralty Dramatic Society, often as *Universal Understudy*. In this production of Rope *(1964) I think I stepped in with a fortnight to go. Luckily I was a quick study. From left Marjorie Imlah, Alan Brookes, Chris Young, Doug Munson, Richard Hill, Clifford Snell, Joan Walsh.*
(Bottom) A spare Flag Officer Gosport-side was always useful for Divisions: inspecting the guard at HMS Daedalus, *1981.*

6 'Green things springing' (p. 97). Clockwise from top left, Lucy and Harriet Hill; Nigel Hill; Tricia, Lucy and Harriet; Eleanor Callcut; Charlotte Thistlewood; Alexandra Callcut; Anna Thistlewood; Richard with Penny Callcut; James Thistlewood.

7 'Green things springing' (p. 97). Clockwise from top left, Lucy and Harriet Hill; Nigel Hill; Tricia, Lucy and Harriet; Eleanor Callcut; Charlotte Thistlewood; Alexandra Callcut; Anna Thistlewood; Richard with Penny Callcut; James Thistlewood.

8 (Top) The family commissioned this cartoon by Charles Miles for my 60th birthday. It looks a bit overdone, but life at the Middle Temple was indeed full of varied interests, as well as a fair whack of work at the day (and sometimes night) job.

(Bottom) Humphrey Lyttelton and his band played at the Middle Temple every year. His lightning cartoon for Tricia crowned one occasion with extra delight.

The Slag Moraine

At the Imperial Defence College the students, in groups, did foreign tours lasting about four weeks and taking in the major countries of one region and, in addition, three-day industrial tours of parts of the United Kingdom. I wrote this in a coach on passage through Wales; it must have been before the Aberfan disaster, for I surely would not have dared to write it after that.

> The Slag moraine grows
> Tins that shine for a year
> Then rust. It goes
> Faster than a glacier.
>
> Faster than glaciers die
> Seeds from grass and trees blown
> Put down roots. Clouds fly,
> Rain makes, desert is sown.
>
> Less than an ice age
> Need pass for a garden
> In this hanged valley.

Administrator to Evangelist

We had a real good hellfire preacher in our parish at Littleton, outside Winchester. I loved his uncompromising stance, but:

> Listening to you preach
> I think what luck you have
> In the luxurious intransigence
> Of the morally brave:
>
> How you can embrace the Good
> Without your least dissent
> Or onus to consider
> What is expedient.

Pakistan, 1965

This is very odd. There we were on tour, fifteen of us from the Imperial Defence College, caught up in a war between the two great states of the Sub-Continent, and there I was writing descriptive poetry about the landscape. Well, I did at the end try to describe what it was like to be there, in the war, and so curiously uninvolved.

I. The Plain

All new, for me,
This heartland: the slow
Pad of bullocks, the red dust.
More miles from the sea
Than I care to count, than I have been ever, go
Rivers great with a century of snow,
Huge, barely tamed. The crust

Of the pink earth suddenly, here and there,
Crumbles, subsides twenty feet, leaves a small cliff
With, beneath, a miniature, flat
Alluvial plain, rich, where
Sugar or maize grow. If
Anyone looked at that

In England he'd think, erosion. But here you can till
Top, sides and bottom; the land
Is as deep as broad, and old
With millennia of tilth, of hand
And beast and plough, war and goodwill,
Heat and cold.

Unnamed birds in unknown trees,
All new, flower into unexpected song;
Said to be parodies
Of other shyer birdsongs further back
In the fields. Along
The roadside march canals, brown and slack,

Arteries of the plain. And, all new,
Across that sea-like plain the hills rise
Miles away, blue.
There it is cool, here the dry heat

Swats down. Pink dust grates on the eyes,
Rising in clouds at each hoofbeat

Of bullock, donkey and horse, each screaming halt
Of madly-driven cars.
               Well, it is true
That this land a thousand miles from the sea
May be old, impersonal, proud, full of fault:
But it is, at the moment, all new
And all for me.

II. Murree

Here, from this hilltop, we look down
Upon more hilltops far below
All treed and green; at night, the glow
Of lights in a far distant town

Reveals the plain. The standard tale
Of Cities of the Plain is here
Reversed: their ethics were severe,
While this hill-station could assail

Most moral postures. High above
The heat, the idle ghosts repine
Of the late centuries' decline:
Colonels' ladies making love

With desperate ingenuity
To subalterns, who in their turn
Hotly, madly pant and burn
Before some chill and virgin She.

(Though now the tourists' tastes reflect
A less robust and certain age).
Meantime, as now the currents rage
Of occupation, war, neglect,

Blank-eyed in front of their bazaars
The hillmen, proud and timeless, stand
Inheritors of this hard land
And spare no thoughts for love or stars.

III. War

The air-raid sirens sound like horns
Of ancient taxis. In the dark
A Bofors pops ridiculous
At the high raiders, from the park.

Voices shout words I do not know
Across the hot night. They, maybe,
Are giving orders. It's no comfort
To know they are not meant for me.

Foreign tongues: and foreign, war
For me, though I was bred to fight;
Not my concern, this. One lone bomb
Shivers the timbers of the night.

I know that it's a tragedy;
Yet oddly distant, like a play
With cardboard characters. The dead
Are dummies. Heroes belt away

Into the blue, and no more real
Than a trapeze. Since this is so
For me, I have no business here;
I've lost my contacts; I must go.

Mostly about Elizabeth of Bohemia

I suppose every poet is allowed one Dark Lady. Mine was an accomplished amateur actress; we struck sparks from each other on the stage and sometimes off it. Thanks mostly to her good sense and moral strength, it never became carnal, no damage was done and the main outcome was the ensuing sonnet.

Someone once asked me, if there was one thing I could leave behind, what it would be. I unhesitatingly replied 'One halfway decent sonnet'; and I think I would put this forward as a candidate, though there are some others in this book that have a claim. Many sonnets tend to sag in the middle, after a sonorous opening and a lift at the end. I don't think this one suffers in that way, partly through the succession of verbs – *assault, glow, impact, burn, stamp, pierce, speak*. Does it tail off into cliché at the end? Well, perhaps. And, of course, 'impact' as a verb is questionable; it is of its period, the sixties, when missiles and moonshots were all the rage. No regrets, damn it, let it stand.

Yes. From her title only, we can trace
Her history. The Winter Queen whose bright
Torch flared one moment in the frozen night
Then, as the breath's mist, faded. All that grace
Gone for a beggar's song into the space
Behind the cold stars. Yet the rivers in light
Frozen, between bare trees, assault the sight:
Yes. In such images she has her place.

I have such winter images that glow
In early darkness, that impact and burn
Imagination: feet that stamp the snow,
Eyes that pierce fog to speak. In winter things
Your place. But will the ghost of you return
Unsought, on summer's roundabouts and swings?

A Birthday Offering

But the more durable bonds remained, and towards the end of my Ministry
of Defence time I began to write birthday verses for Tricia once a year –
with, no doubt, some gaps. Some were, moreover, transient indeed, and
will not sustain publication. This, from the heading of the paper, is the first
that has survived. It must date from 1978 or 1979. It is the only thing I
have ever written in hexameters.

One day of slanting rain seen bright against dark trees,
New lambs on spent sodden grass, the locks still turned on the spring,
But your joy at a patch of snowdrops began to turn the keys
And laughter and warmth by the fire gave us a song to sing.

One day you planned should be mine and you made it so indeed,
Made it so truly and well that I scarcely could turn a phrase
Of thanks; yet I dare to wonder why you felt the need
Since you gave not only one, but so many of your days.

And what, man-like, I give in return is little enough
And tawdry enough, much dross, defaced by worry and rage;
All I can offer, on your one day, is this distant love
– But call it, at least, no other – and some muddled words on a page.

Wall Posters

I explained in the preamble to this chapter how these came about. Some brief description of the circumstances is needed in each case, even though one should not try to explain a joke.

Malta Rundown

In 1977–8 UK defence forces were in the process of leaving Malta where they had been for the best part of two centuries. The plan was known as the 'Malta Rundown' and was necessarily a fairly freewheeling affair, aided by the presence as the last Flag Officer Malta of Os Cecil, probably the most individual character in the RN since the Second World War. We expected him to charm our way out of Malta, and he did.

Os had asked for a Landing Ship Dock (LPD), *Fearless* or *Intrepid*, to be the final naval unit in Grand Harbour. Those of us who knew him thought the main reason for this was that the tank deck of one of these ships was the sort of place he would throw one of his legendary parties, with (if we were not mistaken) a duckpond with live ducks in the landing craft well. Unfortunately neither ship turned out to be available.

The two central characters in the piece are of course fantasy, owing a lot to A.A. Milne. In fact both are communications jargon. RATT was short for Radio Activated Teletype, which ships in harbour were to keep watch on, and TARE the Tape Assisted Relay Equipment back in Boddington, UK, which was the rear link. I found the mention of them in the Defence Council Instructions irresistible – as I did the name of the High Commissioner in the third stanza. The BFBS were the British Forces Broadcasting Service, who were thinking of pulling out early, as I (perhaps mistakenly) recall.

Who planned the Rundown? Nobody knows.
(Under the moon the gregale blows).
But a whisper goes round Castile Square:
It was Harbour Ratt and Boddington Tare.

Where is Dom Mintoff? Off to see
The bad bold Colonel Gaddafi.
Who shall we send to watch him there?
Why, Harbour Ratt and Boddington Tare.

When the BFBS has got the shivers
And to his roots the Aspin quivers,
Who is it stands alert, aware?
Harbour Ratt and Boddington Tare.

When Os steps on board his LPD
And even the ducks prepare for sea,
Arm in arm round Castile Square
Go Harbour Ratt and Boddington Tare.

Turkish Limerick

Most of the jibes in the Wall Posters were about Funny Foreign Names, and
even by extension Funny Foreign Fellows, and I am conscious that this sort
of thing is now regarded as deeply incorrect and potentially offensive. So I
have cut most of them out of this book; if in future years they come back into
fashion, and won't at that lapse of time cause a Serious Diplomatic Incident,
maybe someone will have another look. Meanwhile, one or two surely will
not cause a third world war. One such was the result of a tease from a junior
member of the team, who presented me with the name, and curriculum
vitae, of a new member of the NATO staff – now have a go at this, sir . . .

Mr Achmet Birincioglù
On defence should have more than a clue;
With a Master's in Law
He did Customs before –
So I think he's an expert, don't you?

Square Dance

Uganda was ruled in 1979 by the monstrous Idi Amin, who one day sent
a small force to make an incursion into Tanzanian territory. This called
forth a cry for help not only from the Tanzanian President, Julius Nyerere,
but from our High Commissioner (Mr Moon) in Dar es Salaam, who
suggested all sorts of military aid we might offer. He was backed, without
total conviction, by the Secretary of State for Foreign and Commonwealth
Affairs (D.A.L.O.) and Brian Watkins, the official in charge of the relevant
FCO department. Fred was, of course, Mr Mulley, our own affectionately
regarded Secretary of State. There are a lot of in-jokes here; any historian
of the period who comes across it may care to take a closer look.

I wrote a tune for this one, but it did not appear on the Wall.

Idi was a naughty man who crossed his neighbour's fence
(With a heigh and a ho and a Moon-ee-o)
He caused a situation that was really rather tense
(Please send help very soon-ee-o).

Julius found a Front Line where it didn't ought to be
(And he only had a platoon-ee-o)
So he did a lightning splicing-job on Hands-Across-the-Sea
And he called for help from old Moon-ee-o.

H.E. offered him the Air Force and he offered him the Fleet
(With a DALO, a Watkins and a Moon-ee-o)
And half a tank division just to make the job complete
(November this was, not June-ee-o).

So then cheer up me hearties, for though Fred did not agree
(And please forgive my lampoon-ee-o)
If you wait another fortnight the *Ark Royal*'s going free
(With a diddle and a doddle and a quibble and a coddle
    and a quiver and a quaver and a Moon-ee-o).

Deskby

Apart from the Treasury – who are not a laughing matter, nor would they wish to be – the main Whitehall department with whom we in the Defence Policy Staff worked were the Foreign and Commonwealth Office. Whether one had been in a diplomatic job before, as I had in The Hague, or was new to the milieu, it was a fascinating experience to be in contact with these cultivated, often subtle, always urbane, sometimes quaintly formal people who worked constantly for the country's interest as they saw it – which was not always the way we did.

But they did have their funny little ways, and procedures. 'Deskby' was, and still perhaps is, a prefix on Foreign Office telegrams signifying that they should be on the desk of the appropriate officer in headquarters by a certain time. The piece that follows was triggered by a stern FCO circular insisting that any telegram bearing the prefix must also contain the Date Time Group (DTG) of the dispatch, to help establish priorities.

I shall mount a small coup on some cold autumn day
And set up a republic around Swanage Bay;
All the tinpot ambassadors will come to me
And I'll call my capital Deskby-on-Sea.

At Deskby-on-Sea, at Deskby-on-Sea,
The diplomats' wives may gather for tea;
One small point of protocol, though, I shall name:
Hats will be *de rigeur*, and must all be the same.

I'll devote all my time to confusing the Corps
With draft treaties and mild Declarations of War;
I shall crack all their ciphers, reserving my glee
For 'Deskby by Deskby' – with no DTG.

At Deskby-on-Sea, at Deskby-on-Sea,
My MFA's rules will be not at all free,
And woe to that Embassy casting its vote
For a *bout de papier* when it should be a Note.

For State Visits, the programme will not show its face
Till 3.30 am on the day of the race;
And last-minute amendments that programme bedevil
By telephone call at Third Secret'ry level.

At Deskby-on-Sea, at Deskby-on-Sea,
On one point at least the whole Corps will agree:
A post there can be counted a penance for crime –
But I shall be having the whale of a time.

The Hedgehog and the Elephant

To the surprise of some including me, I was promoted to rear admiral at the end of 1980. There would be one appointment in that rank, the very pleasant one of Flag Officer Admiralty Interview Board at Gosport, in charge of the assessment of candidates – not far short of two thousand a year – for commissions in the Royal Navy, Royal Marines and Women's Royal Naval Service. It was the first 'people' job I had had for many years, but the procedures and criteria were well established and the board members mostly very experienced and perceptive. I hope we picked some good ones and eliminated the dull, the dim and the daft. Of the rejects, the dull by far predominated.

It was a joy to live a decent domestic life after the barbarities of the Ministry of Defence, the artificialities of an Embassy and even the constrictions of HMS *Dryad*. We were allowed a nice house to entertain in and did in fact meet a lot of interesting people, including visiting headmasters, senior officers and civil servants, and academics. We even ran a couple of conferences on Medium Maritime Power.

This must I think be the second of my birthday offerings to Tricia – which became more and more frequent as time went on. Verse with a light touch that makes a serious point is not easy to bring off, but I hope this manages to go some way.

The hedgehog and the elephant are quite attractive both
And very much to be preferred to mantis or to sloth;
But whether in the meadow or beneath the jungle tree
Their incompatibility is very clear to see.

For what hedgehog has not trembled and what hedgehog has not
    shrunk
From the all-too-violent trumpet and the clumsy probing trunk?
And what elephant has failed to quail before the hedgehog's freeze
In the circular position – to say nothing of the fleas?

But the most peculiar aspect of the whole affair is this:
That constantly they undergo a metamorphosis;
For hedgehog turns to elephant, and in that flash of time
The pachyderm in turn becomes a fretful porpentine.

But sometimes they get out of phase, thus into phase perchance;
Incarnate both as elephants they do their stately dance
Or, as hedgehogs both, rub noses with a gentle whiffling sound.
And that's the love, my love, that makes this wretched world go round.

Jack in the Box

Finally in this section, this is the only poem in which our family appears. The first version was written in middle 1960s, and the poem went through several rewrites; this dates from about 1980. In some ways it is the most mysterious thing I have ever done. If asked to explain it, I would be at a loss. Yet it does seem to have something to say. The bad rhymes in the second and third stanzas are half-deliberate; they are half-rhymes after all.

The Word lies like a cube whose walls
Angle the light a thousand ways;
Straight or curiously refracted,
Random or directed rays.

Hugging their secrecies a tribe
Of small emphatic children come
Convinced that this is not unlike
The Word that lives inside the womb;

Hungry for laughs, their present griefs
Need some magician, poet or god
To press the button and release
The Joke that lies inside the Word.

CHAPTER 5

Three Sea Pieces

THE SETTING FOR THESE POEMS, written in 1967, was my final commission at sea in HMS *Duchess* (1960–62) and translation to Ministry of Defence work. This, as I have already suggested, was a time of emotional turbulence mostly vocational in origin. A professional seaman, trained and prepared for sea command, looks forward to fulfilling that function. Being deprived of it, even in the course of promotion to senior ranks, hits hard. I said to myself that I would not complain in prose; but the poetry began knocking about in my head quite soon after I began work in Whitehall.

In fact the opening two poems of the set were more or less direct recollections of situations that occurred in *Duchess* herself. The first was a visit to the Greek island of Mytilene (Lesvos) where, in addition to my normal duties as navigator and staff operations officer, I was temporarily first lieutenant and second in command, because our splendid executive officer Geoff Hammond had injured himself leaving the whaler after regatta practice, and was in hospital. It was a tough time under our exacting captain, and our normally exemplary ship's company, relaxing after a busy exercise schedule, were not quite as well-behaved as usual.

The second poem grew from a task of a different sort; search and rescue, especially if unsuccessful, has its own dark tone and a week of such activity generates particular tensions. They were resolved, as the poem suggests, in a singularly happy way.

The third piece deals directly with my own situation, but echoes no doubt the sentiments of many an officer placed on the 'Dry List'. A lot of them *did* complain in prose (try reading *The Naval Review* for those sixties years); I simply chose to do it in verse. The nostalgia was very real and I am not sure, even forty years later, that I have fully lost it. Someone once said it was a bitter poem; I don't think that is true, but it does not flinch from sadness.

The opportunity to put these feelings into verse form occurred with the Stroud Poetry Festival, 1967. This called for three poems

63

from each candidate of not more than 100 lines each, and seemed to me to provide an incentive for substantial work that could, in the unlikely event of its winning, be spoken before an audience. It turned out that winning was indeed very unlikely, as there were over 900 entries and only three prizes, but I was delighted to be among the thirty or so commended entries, and two of the three poems were published in *Festival Poems* later that year. I was at that time very diffident about using my name, much less naval rank, and assumed the pen name 'Lepidus'. That really was a trifle bitter: those who know their *Julius Caesar* will recall that Lepidus was 'a slight unmeritable man Fit to be sent on errands'.

The structure of the three pieces goes back to my much earlier experiments with musical forms. I had found this a useful discipline in treating complex subjects, particularly where contrasts were involved – as they usually are in any substantial poetic process. Thus the *Sea Pieces* can, without too much stretch of the imagination, be thought of as a sonata in three movements.

The first, *The North Wind*, has two main subjects: the Greek island and the visiting ship. Spanning the two are the north wind itself, that katabatic wind that sweeps down from the cold land in many parts of the Mediterranean; and the ship's officer, preoccupied with the business and safety of the ship yet seeking a full appreciation of the island's atmosphere and culture. If any readers think it worth analyzing the poem in detail, they will I believe find a quite well-defined first-movement form here.

The third movement, *On the Beach*, though subtitled a rondo, is a bit more complicated than the simple A-B-A-C-A that that implies. It is more like the so-called sonata-rondo, where there is more interplay between the themes, which here are the river, the lodging ashore, the office building, traffic on the river and in the street, and memories of the sea, all seen or heard through the eyes and ears of the 'beached' officer.

The second movement is different, and not really in a classical form at all. It is linear in its narrative, and therefore more 'romantic' in form as well as in content. If one wanted a musical analogy, it would probably be a free fantasia, and that is strengthened by the recurrence of one particular word-ending. But there are developments and contrasts within the sequence, and a distinct merging of imagery

towards the end of the poem. By the way, radar echoes do shine, and
there is no inaccuracy in the final line.

I. The North Wind

Few towns face north
In the Aegean. Crookt
In the arms of warm south-facing bays
Those white houses, straight lines and semicircles
Designed by Euclid, stare through the haze
That is spray, whipped
By the north wind, heaping
The steep waves like spode plates,
Ceremonial under the canopy of Greek blue.

The spray that wets, chaps, salts the lips
Offends no well-found ship
Staying to seaward: but with two anchors down
And moored stern-to the town
Quay, then the wind whips
And the surge runs up the bay, snatches
At cables, wires; full on the beam
Takes her, creaking: uneasy the watches
All on the jump, and in the boilers steam
At immediate notice. We make the brightwork gleam
For visiting firemen, but anxiety patches
The cloth of blue.
                        For the good of the service
One hurries to hilltops. Here among yellow
Rocks, bushes that might be tamarisk or oleander
Burn in the white wind;
Stones that may well be stelae
Exhausted lie in the dry afternoon
Telling nothing. A sound that could be syrinx
But is more likely to be saxophone
Bends up the hill from the town, where the crew
Drunk on retsina and pints of ouzo
Are upsetting painted carts; police and townsfolk
To be placated, men to be seen, admonished,
Punished: all the process of the day.
Somewhere, it is easy to see,

Somewhere, it is easy to say,
The message went astray between Greece and me.

Because what Englishman does not believe
That he ought to get from Greece some crown
For the spirit: in the grove some kiss from the leaf
Of myrtle, and that same north wind
Running like wine down the slopes, thrilling like fire?
Some inheritance from the drum and dance,
Bulls and the Lion Gate? I think my chance
Has gone. The lyre
Will scarcely strike for me, only the town
Band at the ship's football match playing execrably
God Save the Queen. Myrtle
Is somebody's girl, and the bull
Is a brass, not a gold, god, polished despite the spray.

So what has happened to the Greek fire?
How much is the bouzouki like the lyre?

Perhaps it is as well that all I have
Of symbiosis is: an Athens café
With one soldier dancing absorbed, alone
And filthy drunk; a bull-faced double-bass
In Herod Atticus playing, of all things, Haydn
With gusto to bust a gut; Santorin
Fearful still under the bright noon;

And of course the wind
That has blown through the centuries
Turning the houses' backs to it, whitening
Woodwork and sea, tempering
Except in sheltered corners, the blare of the sun.

The wind and the salt haze
Slap up the hull, corrode
Grey weatherwork: while ashore, roots hold
Only what the sea dare not erode.

Under the canopy of Greek blue
The ship, with ceremonial awning spread, lies
Uneasy, stern-to
The Town Quay. Wires

Go slack, then taut as the sea
Runs up the bay. Preoccupation, due
Precaution, some anxiety,
And in the boilers the scarcely banked fires.

II. The Sea Beat

After a week off the Smalls, searching
For a downed helicopter and the drowned men
Inside, day and night running
Lines through the cross rips, pinging
On rocks and wrecks till the sea's surging
Was part of the beat of the blood:
        In temporary command,
My stern captain consenting, past Land's End,
And through the chops of the Channel, past Portland –
The guns doing their last firing –
And upharbour to South Slip Jetty, I took her home.

An easy passage for November;
After the plunging seas off the Smalls, an even
And gentle run up Channel, neither clawing
Into an easterly nor wallowing
In a westerly blow; no groping
In fog for radar contact of land or ships;
A lucky passage. But the sea beat
Stayed in my head, the revolving line
Of the radar spun in my eye
With the smudge of the Smalls lighthouse echo creeping
Down the shining index. The daynight glow
Of the Ops Room burned in my brain still, even as burned
In my worn being, the want of you
Only across the town now. By half past nine,
The track charts done, the reports
Drafted and the management
Satisfied for the time being,
I got ashore, hungry and sharp across
The town: to find you gone, out at a party
Down the road. There I tracked you, shining
Among the painted faces, lighting
That drab quarter: now all my being.

Not to be rude, we stayed
Some while: though I am afraid
I was rude, gruff in my wanting.

After, in love, deep in the surges of loving,
The sea beat and the beat of the blood,
The radar's light and dark and the white and gold
That is always you, merged, fused: all my loves
Married at first and last. I was home
And away, a new
Amphibian dredged up from the past
Or the future, a composition
Of all identities that I have been.

But you, still one, a unity of being,
Burned in my night a beacon
With no cross-grain in the tides of your loving.

I slept unwilling and woke shouting
For a bearing of the Smalls. But you there
Only lay easy and long,
Hair like an echo shining.

III. On the Beach: A Nostalgic Rondo

On the river the reed
Vibrates and is still.
Grained by light from the South Bank, the tide
Ebbs towards the dawn, bearing its swill
Of branches, blocks, oil and detergent foam
At three and a quarter knots straining the buoys
Hunched against it and the night.

Overhead in the black ice of night the useless stars
Burn slowly away. Towards morning,
Sweating from a nightmare of navigation
Dangerously ill-performed, from my landsman's bed now
I hear the rattle of chain cable down
A hawsepipe: some North Sea Flatiron coming to rest,
Turning at rest abreast the gasworks,
Swinging to take the flood. Four short, one long
Blast, the signal. On the river the reed
Vibrates and is still.

At a desk in a building by the river
The merciful window faces the street.
Footfalls beat our long retreat
Down clinical passageways. Ravines
Of stone show columns of cars that wheel
At a signal. Under this building, machines
Pulse and roar: one morning
Stumping under umbrella and hat
I saw the belching chimneys: sat
At my desk with a ridiculous whim
To ring down Chiefy and tell him
To stop making black smoke.
                            The rim
Of the crater recedes. It is easy to say
That everything is much the same: home and away,
Land and sea . . . It is easy to say
That the beach has compensations: joys
Of home-not-away, of the gay
Company of like minds, of civil hours
And unpunctured sleep; no boys
Breaking the law and their heads, no powers
To cherish and command. It is easy to say.

On the river the reed
Rides on the still
Flood. The bridge slides
Into the mist.
                That side of Dover Strait
We worked up to full power, then saw the banks
Of fog ahead: hurriedly
Rang down to ease her, picked a delicate
Way past the Varne, anxious, the radar
None too healthy, and sirens,
Our own and others', echoing round the fog.

One glum shape thumping
Its diesel, pushing half the Channel before it,
Lurched past. Cursing we sauntered on
Through that patched evening and uneasy night.

Here headlamps grow in the mist.
A plane-tree drips in the dark.

On the river the reed,
Scarcely visible, rides still.

Not only in lonely streets
Where bare the footfall echoes
Comes the pain. It beats
Where the traffic goes:

At bus stops and crossings
Where the wheels stop, and churn
Again: as a car swings
And his next astern

Turns a fraction inside –
Ease her now, ease,
Come down in speed, swing wide,
Then catch her. Increase
Revs and the rate of turn,
Settle; flash Sorry
To the next astern.

On the river the reed
Vibrates and is still.
No more seas of summer,
Windflowers constant in change,
Clouds answering muster the whole horizon round
– None overhead – and stars
Telling their names twenty minutes after sunset
Falling one by one to the sextant's swing.
Not ever seas of winter
Where yards dive and the shudder and groan
Of rivet and rigging is enough
To remind us what we own.
But sometimes, at a bus stop, an exhaust
Whips at my sense; and it's funnel smoke
Over the bridge, and all the bright destroyers
Stand by to slip in the blue and yellow morning.

So the empty lighter butts at its mooring.
On the river the reed
Vibrates and is still.

CHAPTER 6

Middle Temple and After

THE LUCK I HAVE HAD all my life held especially after I was placed on the retired list. A few months looking for a job during the summer of 1983 were salutary, not least in going genuinely on the dole and seeing the inside of a job centre. They were not idle though, because I was writing my second book, *Anti-Submarine Warfare*, which turned out quite well – helped probably by the fact that I was neither a submariner nor an anti-submarine specialist. I did indeed consider becoming a full-time author, until my publisher pointed out that to make anything like a decent living writing books on naval or maritime subjects, I would have to publish four books a year. 'That would make me a hack', I said. 'Yes', he said.

So inevitably I found myself applying for jobs in the administrative field. Casting the net far and wide – I cannot now remember how bizarre some of the options were – I had few interviews offered, but the best day included two finals: one for the post of Under Treasurer (Chief Executive) of the Middle Temple, and one as Director of the Wilton Park Conferences then (and now) held at Wiston House, Steyning.

The first seemed to go all right; Tricia was interviewed too, and that was worth a lot of points. The second was quite funny in retrospect. I wasn't doing badly, I thought, in front of a group of fairly sophisticated gentry, when the chairman asked 'Now, if conversation got round to cultural matters after dinner, what subject would you hope for?' 'Oh, music', I said. This clearly disappointed them, and one said 'I'd rather hoped you would say modern literature'. Now if I had been quick enough I would have diverted that into poetry, because I could have displayed some knowledge of at least Eliot and Graves and maybe even Larkin and Auden, though I wasn't then too secure on those two. But instead, I took it to mean The Novel and said 'Oh no, I'm afraid you are talking to someone who has never been able to finish a book by either Proust or Anthony Powell'. 'Oh, but', said the chairman 'If you were Director of Wilton Park you'd have *plenty* of time to read Proust'. I might even then have been able to recover by saying 'That was not what I meant at all. That was not it, at all', but remained silent; and thought I detected a distinct rustle of silk handkerchieves.

So it was just as well that I was offered the job at the Middle Temple. This was the start of ten immensely fulfilling as well as pleasant years. One of the four Inns of Court, this is a college of barristers, an ancient institution that in the fifteenth and sixteenth centuries vied with the great universities in its teaching functions and still, at the end of the twentieth, had much to offer in various ways to the legal profession. The governing body was the Masters of the Bench, barristers and judges, people of great intelligence who were also highly responsible in their attitude to running the Inn; but sensibly, they did not choose their chief executive from among their number, employing instead someone with administrative skills to do the day to day functions and head the staff of eighty or so caterers, accountants, students' officers, estate managers and librarians. The centre of the work was finance, as it is in any enterprise; our turnover was about eight million pounds, well within my scope.

So that was now my task, and with it came a delightful flat in that haven between Fleet Street and the River Thames, so that my travelling time was a full forty seconds a day. If at any time in next ten years I considered that I would rather be breaking stones, then I was a most ungrateful fellow. But it happens, of course, and I suppose one could say that the difficult moments arose mainly from questions of power. The Inns were under fairly constant fire from people, mostly at the Bar but sometimes in central or local government, who thought they were self-serving anachronisms and wanted to abolish, radically change or control them. In preserving the institution that I served, I had the advantage of years of Whitehall experience including all the tricks of the defensive; but it was much more palatable to be able, sometimes, to take initiatives – financial, educational and in matters of policy generally. I hope the Inn, and the Inns of Court as a whole, were left in a stronger position than they were when I joined, and one that was more beneficial to the profession of the Bar.

A certain amount of verse was written during this time, as well as five books on maritime subjects. That work, mostly done in the mornings between 6.30 and 8.30, did not, I think, take away from the time I devoted to the Inn; and editing *The Naval Review* was a Saturday-morning job, done at Cornhill House, Bishop's Waltham, where we escaped at weekends. So life was comfortably full, but we were both still full of running and coped. Moreover, there was time to plan and take holidays, and Tricia and I saw far more of the world in those ten years than we had seen before. It was some compensation particularly for her, having had few fleshpots while I was in the navy.

The verse of those years was less concerned with large forms than before. I suppose that to some extent I was more concerned with simple visions, and the complexities that called for such things as sonata-form, though they may have been around, did not occur so frequently or were not, in my view, suitable subjects for poetry. So most of the poems that follow are quite short, follow no coherent theme and contain no narrative – which has never, for me, been a very attractive form anyhow.

Parrots Fighting

This was in a hotel in Bangkok, our first holiday after leaving the navy in 1983. I don't think the poem works very well, but it is the only piece of verse that emerged – although a split pair of trousers on boarding an elephant was more memorable.

On a high perch of vantage
Top bird of three – all-coloured, all fit, alert,
Clearly well-fed – defends that sound position
With beak and claw but most it seems with squawk;
Noise unremitting. Second bird contests,
Third bird looks on. Will they change round tomorrow?
Only they care. It staggers the thought,
This empty controversy every day:
But see, their wings are clipped,
They cannot fly nor forage;
What can they do but quarrel and preen?

Away

One was far more subject to the Paul Gaugin syndrome in the Ministry of Defence than ever subsequently. So, indeed, was Tricia; I was taken to the Boat Show with a mandate to look at something about 36 feet long capable of going round the world. I pleaded that I was dangerous, if not lethal, in any craft less than a hundred feet long and we wouldn't last more than a day or two. But the theme remained in my head, to emerge years later.

To paint nude Polynesians
Sail off into the sunset
Simply to wander the ways
Or live in a tower with some pale girl:

Well, some of us have done it
And found, no doubt, no paradise;
Only a glimpse, rare, at once lost,
No more substantial than birdsong
Fresh in the morning halfheard
After a fretted night.

That, anyhow, is the case
For those of us who have never set out
To paint nude Polynesians.

Spring Sonata

The winter of 1984–5 was unusually hard and icicles hung treacherously from every step in the Temple. Even at the end of March, when Tricia's birthday came along, it was terribly cold. I was now in the habit of writing birthday verses for her – there will be more later – and this sonnet accompanied a record of Beethoven's violin sonata Op.24. I often wondered, when I first encountered it, why this was written in F major, which is quite a long way from the natural key of the violin. But of course (and anyone with any knowledge of composition would have realised it without missing a beat), the first subject starts on a major third, with a sustained note that launches the joyous theme; and naturally Beethoven wanted it to start on an open string, giving the maximum purity of tone. So the A string, a third up from F, dictates the key signature.

It is a measure of my attitude to music that I have always thought this something of a cop-out on Beethoven's part. Some people are never satisfied.

In the north wind the leaves drop off the rose
That shivers clutching at the Temple wall.
Some spring this is: more like the year's dead fall
When buds that surly open quickly close,
Then rot and drop. Even if we suppose
The summer sudden-come with cuckoo-call
And unsought heat, this month hangs like a pall
Upon the year, relict of outraged snows.

So, in default of spring, here is that A
That hangs as the first blossom in the tree
Then falls like petals at the end of May;
This is the statement unperturbed and clear
That says the world is right enough: maybe
The only spring that we shall get this year.

Songs of Authority

Perhaps it was that I was dealing with people of great responsibility, and indeed had been for some years, that made me want to deal with their situation in verse. I had, at one time, thought of writing a whole cycle looking at various aspects of their lives, and there will be vestiges of that treatment in some other parts of this chapter.

I was for years uncertain exactly what people I was writing about. It was not really people in the news; politicians posture, media folk scribble and gabble, celebrities strut, and all have some sort of mucky symbiosis with each other, without (it seems to me) very much real power. Nor was it, on analysis after I had written it, about public servants, even the senior ones who have a good deal of clout. I have concluded that the people I was really writing about were what the Yale Law School calls Authoritative Decision-Makers – the heads of huge corporations, the big beasts behind the administrations of the world's most powerful countries, the very top drivers of science, religions and ideologies: in fact, the people who go to conferences at Davos – or should, but don't.

There is no one to speak for us.
Tyrants in Greece paid good money
For poets to chant their praise: wine,
Oxen, corn in painted carts,
And, no doubt, other delights in kine or kind.
For them, hypocrisy
Was an invention, a seed
Just hybridised, new sown.

We reap it heavy in the ear now,
Shocked up in gossip columns,
Lodged with green shoots of envy, after rain.
Its yeasts move sour and silent,
Erupt, infect, destroy
Tissue: we fear it, but cannot
Do altogether without it, a process
Too like our own workings.

We are, in any case, busy
With what there is to do: days
Filled with decision and policy,
Evenings with plans, meetings.
We do not care if our faces are not known
Up to a point; dullness
Can be an advantage, if not pressed
To include those who matter.

So we avoid the light –
Or, at least, over exposure
To light arranged on our worst sides –
And listen to no songs on our names
Produced by the scurrilous or the profane.
But murmur, to ourselves, in the few
Quiet moments allowed us, our own halt words
Scrawled, bent, across the page.

Mason's Yard

This is very personal and may be thought prejudiced. But I have a real difficulty in understanding why so many people cling to the corporeal when life is extinct. Graves, headstones and scattered floral tributes round the otherwise beautifully kept flower and shrub beds of crematoria all seem to me to be negations of what is supposed to be a spiritual condition. I want no part of it.

Let these stones be. Our lives
Need no interpreter
Which, being dead, survives
Only to show we were.

Surely, if have we must
Any memorial
To dignify our dust
It lies not here at all

But in the lives of those
That we have loved and known;
A seed that lives and grows
That we ourselves have sown.

And if by special grace
We leave some words as well,
Let each lie in its place
Telling what is to tell.

North Cape

1989 saw us go on the *Hurtigruten*, the Norwegian coastal mail and ferry service from Bergen to Kirkenes in the very north. It was a memorable quiet holiday, punctuated by swift runs ashore in the numerous little ports at which we called, often for no more than an hour; superb ship handling and navigation; and occasional booming comments from an American table companion. The land of the North Cape was free of all that.

Earth clothes itself
Where it can. Small perfect forms
Lie close to ground. Trees barked
And leaved stand four stiff inches high
Against the salt wind. Moss clings to rock,
Soil in the clefts bears grass. The cold desert
Is no more barren than the hot:
Life wins.

Exchange and Mart

This was prompted by a remark of Kenneth, Lord Diplock, whose wisdom and humour never deserted him even when crippled by arthritis and surrounded by a terrorist threat that demanded three minders at all times. He was a hunting man among many, many other things.

What dignity it has
The language of these advertisements:
The Entire Horse, the Unentered Filly,
Sound Bay Fifteen Hands.

O Stubbs and Surtees,
A whole economy
Founded on horseflesh, muck and country ways.

Not without elegance its successor,
The Clean Car, the Good Runner,
(Not forgetting the Velour Trim);
A concept of the immaculate?

But coper and salesman
Know coarser language;
Bad teeth, gone fetlock, broken wind,
Noisy tappet, bald tyre, shaky rings.

Justice

Though this sprang from a particularly sad situation at the Middle Temple, it deals with a general problem and fear. I don't know which is more terrifying, the prospect of going gaga oneself or of someone very close in the same condition. But most painful of all must be the situation described in this poem – and the self-doubt that it must inevitably bring, along with the sympathy, agony and helplessness.

She's turned against him: shocked voices
Discuss, discuss. *Such a sweet woman,*
Devoted couple, so sad: now she crouches railing
At the stooped judge who was and is her husband.

But he's a saint, does everything for her
And still she'll curse: senile dementia
Makes no distinction as to class or rank.

It's changed her character – and yet, and yet
May he, fair upright judge, consider
What is the true, what was the false, face;
What if for years behind the charm lay
Hate for this man who took you
Got you with child and tied you to a house
Then made you entertain his boring friends;
Preferment gained, then used you as a front
For more preferment . . . And now you strip him
Of his authority where no writ runs
And where he's no defence: wounding,
Measureless, merciless, irresponsible;
Sad chance, just retribution, who can tell?

So he goes home, the justice of appeal,
To where his dribbling wife spits judgment on him:
Who is this man, I did not ask him here,
Send him away, I do not like him now.

Sanctuary by Numbers

Quite suddenly, we are back to astronomical navigation again, and the perils of authority (a little authority) as well. People at the Middle Temple often said to me 'This must be very different from your life in the navy'. I always said it was not so very different; sometimes I added that it was like running a rather grand shore establishment. But this was a slightly altered take on the matter.

When the stars had been taken prisoner
About civil twilight and told me
Time and elevation (no more needed,
The stellar equivalent, let us suppose,
Of name, rank and official number)
Then it was right to go down
To the quiet charthouse and swim
For half an hour in the clean stream of figures,
Corrections, intercepts, position lines.
Out of that purity reject all pleas
From signals, exercise reports,
Tactical conference, movement on the screen:

The safety of the ship demands it:
Sorry sir, I am switched to navigation.

Thus Aristotle
Grappling with the theory of Justice
Fled with relief into proportionate graphs.

So now in a not-so-different world
Fed up with the untidiness
Of vested interest, prejudiced illogic,
Decisions, policies unreconciled,
Irreconcilable: then it is joy
To escape into the figures,
Get clear away to an account's precision
Or generate a cash flow diagram,
Delighting in a logical prediction,
A steady course, an accurate position.

Haiku

I am not sure if I am in tune with the Haiku form, fashionable though it is. It may be possible in Japanese to produce a poem of seventeen syllables with sufficient cadence to resonate with the subject and the thought it contains; but this is in my experience almost impossible to achieve in English.

The first two of these are about cricket: the first villagey and trying to be atmospheric, the second a word of advice that might benefit our national team in this year 2009. The rest spring mostly from a visit to New Zealand in 1994.

End of the Season

Green dusk. White figures
Rope off the square, depart:
Another summer gone.

Yorkshire

Head down, smell the ball,
Bat straight, graft away, never
Cut before July.

Cold War Over

The Russian General
Lopsided with medals
Leans into the void.

Southland

Chill distant mountains
Gather clouds about their shoulders
As evening comes.

Library

Fugitives from life
Flit down avenues of shelves,
Hide in books' covers.

P.A.H.

You fill my thoughts
As, in spring, snow water
Fills the dry river courses.

Ravel

Litter of sound,
Spent blossoms on dry grass?
No; the pattern exists.

Inscription for a Tree

The tree and the word
Live for us: each in its kind
Seeding the future.

Encounter, Te Anau

Also in New Zealand, on going through Te Anau we heard of a rare bird in an enclosure there, a takahe. To our surprise it came and looked at us, and Tricia spoke kindly to it. It is flightless, about chicken-sized and if it was in flocks no one would give it a second thought; but it is notoriously shy, solitary, and its behaviour gives it more than a little charm.

I make no apology for playing about with the sonnet-form, substituting four-foot lines and four-line rhymes for the usual Shakespeherian. The result seems to fit the light-hearted yet courtly effect I wanted to achieve.

Will you allow me, please, to say
How greatly I admired the way
That you addressed the takahe
Which we encountered yesterday?
From all that I then saw and heard
Your most serene and gentle word
Encouraged that embarrassed bird
Whose gestures verged on the absurd;
It grew in confidence; it prinked
Its step; its cheeks glowed newly pinked.
Cause and effect are surely linked:
Thus birds are saved from being extinct
And all endangered species owe
A debt to those that speak them so.

Lake Fletcher

Lost time before, during and after conferences is a common experience. Sometimes, as in Pakistan in 1965, it drags out; another occasion was waiting for a cheap flight out of Halifax N.S. in 1994. It tends to result in verse.

Headstones turn backs to the road
All seemly;
Inscriptions face the church
Though one, no doubt the founding fathers',
Parades its dead to the passer-by.

Houses stand back from the road,
Stare nothing-to-say,
All seemly;
But what dark passions may those windows hide?

Probably not a lot;
This, after all, is Nova Scotia,
Where traffic halts for the walker,
All seemly.

Waverly

Another from the same occasion, a walk in another direction.

Indigenous or introduced
(Which, no one here can tell me)
Roadside flowers are familiar
To the point of irritation.

Introduced but modified,
Language shows oddity:
The Waverly Convenience
Is not what the English think,
Nor what the States would call it,
A Drug Store.

Mostly indigenous,
That animal at the end of a long chain
Outside the petrol (or gas) station
Is much more wolf than doggie;
It keeps quiet, and so do I.

The Guard

This comes from three sources. The first was Allan Heyman, a Middle Temple Treasurer of Danish extraction, who would have taken the last two or three lines as a given solution to dynastic problems in any northern kingdom. The second was Vladimir Nabokov, whose *Pale Fire* put forward very much the same thesis from a different viewpoint. The third was the well-known dialogue: *Reporter:* What are officers for? *Sergeant of Foot Guards:* Teach us how to die, sir.

Fighting was not their business, by and large;
Only to die within the palace after
The gates fell in before the rabble's charge,
Red bonnets, bloodied billhooks, bitter laughter.

But mostly it was quiet before the gates;
The pipeclayed sentries stood, officers twirled
Moustachioes, retired to their estates,
And so the gleaming kingdom faced the world.

They had their power though: when the times were hard
Or the succession failed, it was alone
The Preobrazhensky Regiment of the Guard
That said which Romanov should have the throne.

Fashion and faction: so careers were made
And the elite upheld the dynasty.

But one might get the final accolade:
The young upstanding ranker thought to be
Possessor of a sturdy peasant gene
(The king being inbred, impotent or queer)
Sent to the summerhouse to screw the queen
In order that the state should have an heir.

The Rivers of Mars

A holiday in Morocco in 1998 or thereabouts was one of our least successful, partly through unseasonal rain and flooding. But it brought back some Arian thoughts stemming from our close March birthdays, linked with the raw landscape.

This hungry water
Red with the land's blood
Knifing through all that the goats have left,
Making toothed ranges
As currents meet
In their new channels –

This hungry water
Could be the rivers of Mars
Age-long ago in an angry planet
Aching to bury its water
To sleep its red sleep
Into the nova.

So for us both
Who have relation with Mars
It is right that we saw
That hungry water
Eroding, knife-sharp, descending
To plain, fertile for a generation.

Two Birthday Conundrums

I said earlier that there were not so many complexities at this time. Perhaps it would be more accurate to say there were not so many contrasts, so many tensions between one kind of life and another, such as there must inevitably be for a sailor. But the intellectual complexities were still there, and as incapable of solution as Fermat's last theorem. In the nineties Tricia, with a mind well superior to mine in mathematics and logic, was into chaos theory and cosmology, and it was her interests that triggered the next two poems, for birthdays in 1996 and 1999. The second of these followed solo pilgrimages by me in pursuit of the life of Lord Lewin, who before he died had asked me to write his biography – which I did, I hope faithfully.

I

Blake's God with his dividers
Drew the horizon's rim,
And all the old dimensions
Owed fealty to him.

But we – eternal sceptics
By current theory nerved –
May question these equations
And say that space is curved,

Perspective gently bending
Into a path of light
That swings away unending,
Certain and infinite;

And while by mortal physics
With every global spin
Horizons gather darkly
And threaten to close in,

We shall reverse the process:
Shamble into a run
And make it to the hilltop
To get our blaze of sun:
Till all is said, and done.

II

Is it the linear road, the measured mile,
Or the chaotic vision's wayward dance
Around some vortex half-revealed by chance
Then lost to sight? Now does the beckoning stile
Lead winding to a thicket; or beguile
Without dissembling, through a brave advance
On sound Newtonian principles, to prance
In proud dressage with a top-hatted smile?

You reconcile them both. The tunnel vision
Is not for you. All the old simple laws
Are seen by you to go beyond precision
Into a wilder logic, where the flaws
That lead to chaos have their own volition.
You see them whole. You are our saving clause.

On the Road Back

It was a toss-up whether to include this sonnet. It was written for Tricia's birthday in 2000, after a very long flight from Eastern Australia to Johannesburg. If it shows anything in the line of poetry, it is that the Petrarchian form, once embedded, can be achieved very rapidly at call, whatever one's state of exhaustion.

The other side of earth, the North Reef's loom
And tradewind in the casuarina tree:
Now new horizons make the prospect free
For this immediate time, this bubble-flume
Before they dwindle to a single room.
Blue is the desert colour of the sea,
We must remember; and in honesty
You do not wish to see the desert bloom.

So as it comes, the end of this long day,
Then may tomorrow see the prospect clear
And limping sonnets halt their words away
To greet a day that we should hold most dear;
To say, as simply as one ought to say,
I wish you this and many a happy year.

Villanelle

I have always found this a fascinating form, and the wistfulness to which it lends itself becomes more seductive the older one gets.

At least for rest, if not for peace,
Without much sense of duty done,
I ask my lords for my release;

I saw no grail or golden fleece
And make no claim to battles won;
But look for rest, if not for peace.

The hammers of the world increase,
Percussive-falling, strike and stun;
I ask my lords for my release.

It is too much to ask they cease?
As vain perhaps to ask the sun
To check his raging for our peace.

I do not need the thought police
To tell me I have had my fun
And no parole before release;

Yet still for rest, if not for peace,
Without much sense of duty done
And with no claim to battles won
I ask my lords for my release.

Two Sonnets for Shirley Sherrard

Shirley, wife of Master Michael Sherrard QC, most imaginative of the Treasurers of Middle Temple in recent years, told me at dinner that she was a fellow sonneteer, and we set up a contest, with Lamb and Flag (the Middle Temple emblem) as the subject. I said I would do Shakesperian while she did Petrarchian, and was later upbraided for my lack of chivalry – so I did another, Petrarchian, to make amends.

I. Lamb and Flag

Lady, be sure that I have not forsaken
The challenge that you threw across the floor,
Sonnets at twenty yards. The odds are taken;
The gage accepted . . . I need ten lines more.
Shall I in Lamb and Flag find any rhyme?
Symbols at once of gentleness and zeal
Picked up by chance in some remoter time
And made the image of our common weal?
No; but this observation comes to mind:
Those effigies that round our courtyards keep
Their watch in metal or in stone, I find
Not so much lamb as shrewd experienced sheep.
So, nine-tenths done, striving much less to win
Than to survive, limps this frail vessel in.

II. On Listening to the Poet Laureate and Friends,
On the Topic of the Sonnet, Radio 4, 9 December 2000

Sparked into Motion by the midnight muse,
How can one Cope, forsooth, with such a time
When every Jo can try to make a rhyme
And sets out lists of words from which to choose?
It seems, indeed, there is a widow's cruse
Of endings, banal, workaday, sublime,
Proferred by the wide hats of verbal crime
Making an offer I cannot refuse.

Incestuous pride! Poems on poetry
Are merely navel-gazing, for the nonce;
The eagles mock me from their sunlit crags:
Chaucer to Auden pelt me with a sea
Of mighty images, and call me dunce,
And leave me struggling with our Lambs and Flags.

Bad Theology
On listening to the B Minor Mass

I have no faith. The simpler forms are too woolly, the more complex too unsustainable in logic. I go to church with the oldest liturgy available, and read the Epistle, not so much a fail-safe policy as a feeling that Pauline morality is a reasonable basis for decent conduct (although strictures against fornication sound oddly when addressed to a congregation whose average age is nearer 80 than 70). I also used to go out of respect for the then Vicar of Shedfield, the late Geoffrey Morell, as near approach to a saint as is comfortable. This poem is for him.

Praying eyes should not seek to see
But, as you elevate the Host,
I wonder if you have like me
A soft spot for the Holy Ghost.

The Father's purposes obscure,
The Son's straight aim upon the hip:
So, doubtful, timid and unsure,
Some settle for that Fellowship.

And Bach, at least, paid Him his due
Who, when the Gloria was set,
Gave the *cum sancto spiritu*
His most triumphant music yet.

The Old Soldier at Communion

This is based on real observation, though it has been embellished and owes a good deal to extrapolation. I don't know if the subject really was an old soldier, but he bore himself like one.

Too proud to receive the cup
In his place, he would set out
(The Host once offered) on a planned advance
To the altar, his start line
Well calculated for timely arrival
At the objective; his route
Up the flank aisle, past the traps of the altar steps,
Each tiny shuffling pace a logistic move:
And all the congregation shared the pain
Of that long pilgrimage.

After he had his hip done
He joined the common queue.

The Administrators

Most people who have got to any sort of seniority in any fair-sized organisation spend most of their time doing administration, and not much of it thinking about what it is they are doing or what they are trying to do. It is no surprise that I wrote this several years after ending my work at the Middle Temple, though in my defence I had thought a bit about it in earlier times, and fought through the thickets of bureaucracy to the simplicity of the last three lines. It is another Song of Authority, I suppose.

What is administration? Asked
A certain law student, bright
With a drink or two, tempting,
Seeking to justify himself.

I murmured something trite
About oiling wheels, moved on;
But, as one does, recall now
What I did not say.

It is gravel behind the eyes
At half past three in the morning, churning
Words to a form that will persuade the Board,
Butter to suit my works; marshalling
Numbers for tidy balance on parade:
Figures beneath the uniforms more complex,
Lousy in parts no doubt, but fit to fight
When the audit comes.

It is the queue by day
Of tasks that others might do, but will not
In time or with judgment, and always
That sensation that whatever is in hand
Now, one is taking the easy line
While matters of more difficulty press
At the door, demand attention,
Indeed priority . . .

And the small green men on my shoulder,
Chief Petty Officers, Sergeant Majors,
Saying *You can do better than that, my son,*
Pay attention to detail.

But (in the phrase) there is more:
It is to look for order
In the designer-chaos, to reverse
Entropy simply because
To know where you are (even if it is thigh-deep
In manure) is safer than the void,
The directionless gulfs of unknowing,
The infinite choice of n-dimensional spaces.

And there is more:
It is to listen
For the cracked voices calling from the rubble
And find for them some fair
Tunnel that leads to air,
Without (and have we taken
Too little care of this?) that condescension
That builds another cage, a tighter prison.
So to sum up
(For the Executive Summary
Must always be there, on a different-coloured page
For busy men with but a moment to read):
It is to build a place where
The spirit can flourish:
Our sole justification.

Reels

Scottish Country Dancing has become a recreation. For me, it is scarcely dancing, but I usually move to the right position; which, after years of embarrassment, is an improvement. Tricia does dance, and this poem is for her.

I stood confused till time should reveal
Patterns living inside a reel,
Rhythms in which the bobbins spin,
Corners and eight-bar discipline:
Seeing at last the tribes' wild vigour
Codified, roaded by Scottish rigour.

Quite else for you as the patterns swirled
Around you into your dancing world;
Natural for you the heel-and-toe
And the floor where the foursomes whirling go:
Hair in place but eyes flying,
Freed by the dance from the day's dying.

Round

It is one of those things that must have been done before, but I am not conscious of ever having read such work. In this set, each poem begins with the final line or lines of the previous one, but the subject matter, form and mood of each is quite different. One could say that it is a much compressed four-movement piece, but perhaps a suite is a more appropriate analogy.

There is an underlying theme; put pretentiously, it is Truth – in music, science, education, and visual art. In each case the vision is austere, though at one point that is tentatively questioned.

The first three poems were written in the 1960s, and needed the fourth to cap them. The opportunity came in 2002 from a remark of the Headmaster of the Ichiyo School of Ikebana, Akihiro Kasuya, in conversation with Tricia. She is the President of the UK Chapter of that School and herself a most distinguished arranger, with a succession of Gold Medals at Royal Horticultural Society shows to prove it. Akihiro's remark was to the effect that flower arranging is a transient art: but none the less valid, in its perfect moment, for that.

I. Listening to Brahms

Building such images
As clouds, as castles,
As seas, cages
This music's truth.

Even concepts
As valour, urge,
Nobility, move
The wrong way, divert
This music's truth.

Judgments on tempo
Or technique, go
Only to corrupt
This music's truth.

I shall not repent.
Silicon's impurity
Colours the ruby.

II. The Laser

Silicon's impurity
Colours the ruby
That, shocked, selects
One discrete ray
No bias deflects;
Compassing between minute limits
The pure flute notes of light.

III. The Death Garden:
Soviet War Cemetery, East Berlin, 1966

The pure flute notes of light
Shed through the young leaves
Of birches. Left and right
Granite pillars. The stone grieves

For dead who should have been
By their lights, godless. No,
I do not find this obscene –
But troops of children go

Through the garden without
Laughter or naughtiness
Or ghost of a shout.
Serious teachers press

Dogma and doctrine on
Sixes and sevens. All day
When one troop has gone
Another comes this way.

The air of spring breathes,
Echoes each earnest lie;
Fades. On the wreaths
Broken, the flowers die.

IV. Ikebana

Broken, the flowers die
Like all that has lived; but in the short meantime
Between entity and dissolution, are given
Form on the way to formlessness,
Discipline before the last disorder,
Harmony and contrast of colour and line.

And how one likes one's branches
Owes nothing to cheap symbols
But the truths of shape and the vibrations of colour:
Makes no comment on the commentaries
Seeking a shallower meaning,
Building such images.

Old Man in Garden

In this sonnet, I return to the kind of variation that occurred in the very first in this collection. But in this case the eighth line, instead of leading the final six as in *The Parnasse*, acts as a link between the two sections. The first (1945 – good heavens) may have been fortuitous, but the second (2005) is deliberate, and for me is a valid variant of the Petrarchian form, which can suffer from too distinct a division between the sections.

The old man could be me, or any old fellow. The last line took either two days, or six years, or a lifetime, to write.

Tidying up, he says. That may be right;
Order that comes from long experience
Setting and tending, years of tough defence
Against the weed, the thrip, the cabbage-white,
Putting the powers of anarchy to flight;
A humble goal for half a life's expense –
All tidied up. That is his recompense.

Yet it is he that keeps the borders bright.

It is an image overdone but true –
A song, however trite, still worth the singing –
That old hands rough to touch can yet endue
The seed with force, something like last love bringing
A celebration making nature new:
A grey dry host among these green things springing.

CHAPTER 7

A Light on Shore

THIS WAS WRITTEN LATE IN LIFE, and probably shows it in (often unconscious) recall of past times. The very title and theme are indicative of a less crowded world, and sea. But there always was, and perhaps still is, something evocative about the phrase, and it is not a bad lead in to a nostalgic piece.

It is in four movements, but less of a sonata than a set of variations. Nevertheless there is some echo of musical forms; the second movement is a very dark *adagio*, while the third tries to do the impossible in replicating the apparently rhythmless dance of fishing-boats' lights seen from a ship's bridge. The fourth is a rondo, where I set myself a challenge in writing three Petrarchian sonnets – with intervening episodes – all with the same rhyme endings but of quite different character one with another. I don't know if it comes off, but it was fun to do.

In the first movement, one word will be known to sailors but perhaps not to other readers. 'Clacker', as defined in the classic dictionary *Jackspeak*, means girls. I don't like footnotes, so this must serve in lieu.

I

Lying at single anchor
In the still bay, good holding ground
And shelter in a blow – the hills around
Lean in, treed, dark. Past the next point the glow
Of the town where the watch ashore
Are testing booze and clacker,
But here a different matter:
Halfway up the dark hill
A single light, steady, but through trees
Seen with a branch's random interruption
As the wind, the lightest wind, shifts the leaves.

The watch on board observe
(Having little else to do
Than run the boat routine
And welcome back, later, the half-tipsy
With their new-gotten, old-as-sailors, lore)
That single light on shore
And spell their fantasies
To the burning stars, remote unreal lights
Compared with this:

Simply a street-light on a corniche road?
No, surely not; why one, why not a string?
Porch-light above a hosted door? Perhaps,
But scarcely for this ship's new-welcoming.
Or could it be (the Quartermaster's choice)
The fabled widow with the white Rolls-Royce?

Well, let the dreams run on. In the alchemist's study
Bright before his eyeshade, stirring
Where gold is nearly but nearly there; the light by the pool
Where huge fish observe the stars
Through the water's prism, then resume
Whatever it is their fish-sense tells them: or a sanctuary
Where the Lady of the Sea looks out
Blessing all mariners, keeping her light night-long.

Soon enough it will be time
To turn to other lights, the riding-lights,
The returning boat's lights, lights inside the ship,
With only a swift glance at the single light
Still steady on shore.

The coda is clear: this was fifty years ago
At least, and now you will have the glow
And play of a hundred lights and more
On any hill in a bay ships care to know,
And will have to look elsewhere in your cluttered store
For the fantasies that spring from a light on shore.

II

Uplit the hawk faces
Bones bleak under taut skin

Stretched by privation: hunger for sure
But for more, more,
More than pickings: for loot,
For a dream of jewels,
A world more than rich.

The flickering pitch
On the cliff, ready near the black end of night
To flare into false light
On the false beacon, shifted two miles to the west
Of a true landfall: a homing Indiaman
Sighted at sea last twilight, fishermen
Returning with news, the predators busy
With preparation, ready to turn
The Dodman back to the Deadman, as before.

And the sharp rocks offshore,
Manacles ready to close, at half tide falling,
On the ship embayed: no need for storm,
A southwest topsail breeze enough
For that false fatal landfall. On the beach

Some boats drawn up, to reach
Out to the wreck on the next rising tide:
Knowing the ground
To a foot, there at false first light
To round up exhausted survivors,
Murder them for their rings.

III

Trapani to Marsala
With the Isole Egadi: some title
For a chart, evoking
For the clacissist, Alcibiades
And failed ambition; for the navigator
Chasing the outer arc
Of the Sicilian football;
And for the watchkeepers
Of the middle and morning,
The dance of the lights.

Fishing;
Lifting and dipping
Acetylene flares
Sudden, lost and refound;
Thought safely past
Then another
Right in the grain;
Hauling,
Voices calling
From the lit dark:
The ship avoids
Each hazard as presented
Hoping
No snag for the screws, for the lights
May be on floats,
Supporting nets extending
From parent boats:
Lit or unlit
Or partly seen, dancing
In a pattern not discerned
From the bridge.

Here is no rhythm to the dance
Or rather, no detectable beat
For the simple ear: no doubt
Experts in wave motion could devise
A formula full of complex functions
To explain the dip, the lift, the light, the dark;
But the simple eye
Like the simple ear, will remain unconvinced.

Yet in all the random dance
There shines like a bagpipe's drone
One light undipping, unlost,
Constant: but this must be
A shore light, a light on the point,
The west point of Sicily, rounded
By millennia of seafarers: no great matter
Of shoals or dangers, so the light on shore
Is here but a moment's comfort, before
Return to the more pressing question:

Bobbing
Dipping then relocated
Or seen anew: particles
In a cloud chamber, vanishing
At the moment of observation: flares
On dark faces
Passed uncomfortably close,
And always the dance,
Seeming spasmodic, a pattern
Not understood by the simple ear or eye.
One does the best one can
Avoiding trouble.

IV

The screaming relict of a gale that tore
The sea to tatters, made the halyards sing
Then slat like rifle fire, betokening
Some glaring menace deep within the core
Of earth, the final clap that comes before
The blinding last, the end of everything:
This is our morning watch, that still will fling
Its fury, tear to shreds the rags we wore.

Thus we, come up all bleary from below,
Seeking a track of true security,
Lock on the transit, proof against the tow
Of storm and tidal stream, anxiety
For once allayed, find comfort in the glow
Of lights-in-line that lead us home from sea.

★

Maggiore

The Grand Hotel *et*
Des Iles Borromées
Looks out with thirties eyes
And minimal surprise
At passionate affairs
Begun on wrought-iron chairs
As shingled heroines
Savour, yet fear, their sins.

While seventy years have ranged
Nothing too much has changed;
The necklaces of light
Shine, by a touch, more bright,
But still their spirals take
Reflections from the lake . . .
Nostalgia: one more day
Aux Iles Borromées!

★

Occulting: means the time of light is more
Than that of darkness in each cycle's swing;
A complex word for such a simple thing
It seems at first – but wait, if we explore
The nuances, this light upon the shore
Has much to offer for our journeying;
That steady beam upon the compass-ring
With but a flash of darkness, shuts the door

On one uncertainty at least, that no
More light at all will come, that entropy
Will suddenly cry halt to all the slow
Majestic march of life: we may agree
More light than dark is good, occulting's glow
Across the dangers of our fractured sea.

★

Minore

Earth's veins stretch out
In lost galleries
Deep under sea:

If there were light
It would reflect
Still standing water,
Picks standing sentry;

Abandoned work
Unobserved so forgotten:
For here no light
In the unvisited dark.

★

Going on eighty, I still keep in store
Excuses for a sonnet, figuring
That the established forms can sometimes sing
To novel melodies, and that the score
Of orchestration offers up galore
New textures for familiar fingering:
So now, from all my wayward voyaging,
I turn again to you, my light on shore.

We have no cause to scorn the plants that grow
From old and treasured roots, nor yet to see
Anything false in our quiet embers' glow.
All's steady yet: from falling keep us free,
Even the humdrum has some worth to show,
And so, my dear familiar, let it be.

CHAPTER 8

Epilogue

THERE IS NOT MUCH MORE TO SAY. This has been an account of one man's relation with words, and ideas, and the sea, and (to an extent the paucity of which ashames me) people, and if somewhere the poems can strike a reader with new insights, new cadences, then it will have been a worthwhile enterprise. There could be more, there are still words and phrases and forms buzzing around in there, but in the way of things, not much; it is only the most towering characters that can produce final work like Beethoven's late quartets, *The Tempest*, or Strauss's Four Last Songs, and I am not of that company. I suppose what is more cause for regret is the amount of decent stuff that one could have produced earlier, given more time or energy. Time then for a wistful

Envoi

What could have been
Is, as the mind's eye sees;
Lives: but poorly as a ghost, keening
How fair and brave a thing
It could have been.

Index of Titles

A Birthday Offering	56
A Light on Shore	98
A Place	50
A Sonnet from the East	41
Administrator to Evangelist	51
Anchor Watch, Force 9	17
Away	74
Bad Theology, on Listening to the B Minor Mass	92
Campo	14
Conference Hotel	50
Deskby	59
Downs, Dorset	16
Encounter, Te Anau	83
Envoi	105
Exchange and Mart	79
Fear	2
Final Movement from A Consort of Viols	8
For a Parting	6
Grey Morning at Greenwich	5
Haiku	82
Ikebana	97
Jack in the Box	62
Justice	80
Lake Fletcher	84
Landfall	22
Listening to Brahms	95
Malta Rundown	57
Mason's Yard	78
Mostly about Elizabeth of Bohemia	55
Noise in the Mountains	24
North Cape	79
Nuages	30

Of Age   19
Old Man in Garden   97
On the Beach: A Nostalgic Rondo   68
On the Road Back   89
Owl Eyes   21
Pakistan, 1965   52
Parrots Fighting   74
Prayer   3
Reels   94
Round   95
Sanctuary by Numbers   81
Shot Marshes   21
Spectator   18
Songs of Authority   76
Spring Sonata   75
Square Dance   58
Sunset on London River   4
The Administrators   93
The Barnacle Song   42
The Death Garden: Soviet War Cemetery, East Berlin, 1966   96
The First Point of Aries   33
The Guard   85
The Hedgehog and the Elephant   61
The Laser   96
The North Wind   65
The Old Soldier at Communion   92
The Parnasse   1
The Rivers of Mars   86
The Sea Beat   67
The Slag Moraine   51
The Song of the Over-promoted Cricketer   38
Turkish Limerick   58
Two Birthday Conundrums   87
Two Sonnets for Shirley Sherrard   91
Ultima Thule   7
Villanelle   90
Waverly   84

Index of First Lines

A stately figure in the Dorian Mode   5
After a week off the Smalls, searching   67
All new, for me   52
At least for rest, if not for peace   90
Blake's God with his dividers   87
Broken, the flowers die   97
Building such images   95
Chill distant mountains   82
Dead in these forgotten marshes   21
Earth clothes itself   79
Evidently a winter place   50
Few towns face north   65
Fighting was not their business, by and large   85
For once with time to spare   50
Fugitives from life   82
Green dusk. White figures   82
Grey shoreline seen through the scud, and waves all tattered   17
Head down, smell the ball   82
Headstones turn backs to the road   84
Here are long downs that stretch   16
Here, from this hilltop, we look down   53
I do not say I would not have you change   41
I shall mount a small coup on some cold autumn day   59
I stood confused till time should reveal   94
Idi was a naughty man who crossed his neighbour's fence   59
Indigenous or introduced   84
In the north wind the leaves drop off the rose   75
Is it the linear road, the measured mile   88
Lady, be sure that I have not forsaken   91
Let these stones be. Our lives   78
Listening to you preach   51
Litter of sound   83

Lying at single anchor   98
Mr Achmet Birincioglu   58
Noisy at times and yet quiescent, I   18
Now that a season of twilight   34
On a high perch of vantage   74
On the river the reed   68
One day of slanting rain seen bright against dark trees   56
Over broad acres   30
Praying eyes should not seek to see   92
She's turned against him. Shocked voices   80
Silicon's impurity   96
Since once on a yellow afternoon   38
Sparked into Motion by the midnight muse   91
The air raid sirens sound like horns   54
The bottom of the Albion   43
The evening is heavy   19
The hedgehog and the elephant are quite attractive both   61
The lotus caught your daytime, and the flowers   1
The other side of earth, the North Reefs loom   89
The pure flute notes of light   96
The Russian General   82
The screaming relict of a gale that tore   102
The slag moraine grows   51
The slow/Unbroken rhythm of the conch   4
The tree and the word   83
The Word lies like a cube whose walls   62
There is always the fear   3
There is no one to speak for us   76
There is noise in the mountains   24
This hungry water   86
Tidying up, he says. That may be right   97
To paint nude Polynesians   74
To those who think but do not care   21
Too proud to receive the cup   92
Trapani to Marsala   100
Twice I have seen his face within a wave   2
Uplit the hawk faces   99
Visitors come here often from the lost region   9

What could have been   105
What dignity it has   79
What is administration? Asked   93
When the stars had been taken prisoner   81
When on the Gulf Stream of our richer years   7
When we have said goodbye   6
Who planned the Rundown? Nobody knows   57
Will you allow me, please, to say   83
With no rudder or sail   22
Yellow land   15
Yes. From her title only, we can trace   55
You fill my thoughts   83